Run For The Kitchen

Published by
Charles McCormick

A little sunshine, fresh air
and a good workout brings out
the star in all of us.
This book is dedicated to each and
all of us who know and enjoy that.

Acknowledgements

First, there are the runners who unselfishly shared their time and kitchen wisdom in this endeavor to perpetuate their sport.

Jane Baldridge of Artspeaks assisted by Katie Bucek and Sarah Raykes who orchestrated an impressive attack on the volumes of recipes, photographs and letters ultimately blending the art and the words into a great finished work.

Robert A. Little, president of Wilmington Printing Company, whose insight and wisdom brought this collection to print.

Pete DeVita whose foresight and interest significantly advanced the project.

Finally and perhaps most importantly, the "Unknown Runner" to whom without the likes of you, this book would not be possible nor would it matter.

Table of Contents

Foreword

This project began when a hungry runner woke up late one Saturday morning with a taste for something different.

Various ideas of acquiring good recipes were entertained. After much thought and deliberation, flyers were drafted and thousands were distributed within news letters of running clubs strategically located throughout the United States. Another thousand individual letters were addressed to race directors, coaches and athletic coordinators requesting their personal favorite recipe for review and possible publication. From the time the first flyers went out, hundreds of letters of encouragement, compliments of the project and all kinds of recipes along with requests for finished copies of the book have come in from athletes of all levels. Although each one was very much appreciated, it was not practical to try and publish all of them in one book. What you hold in your hands represents the best. Run for the Kitchen was "written in their own words," and may well be the most outstanding printed collection of runners recipes in existence.

Saturday Morning

Saturday Morning

Fast Track Omelette

"After the Run" Banana French Toast

Eagle Kountry Breakfast Casserole

Arizona Eggs

Oatmeal Crunch

Belgium Waffles

Cantina Eggs

Chicken and Spinach Quiche

Monster Cinnamon Rolls

La Have Scones

Gramma's Rice Pudding

Fast Track Omelette

INGREDIENTS:

1 lb. cleaned & cooked shrimp
4 lrg. eggs
1/4 cup whole milk
dash pepper
dash salt
6 leaves fresh basil
1 Vidalia onion
3 tsp. sugar

Quinoa:
1 cup quinoa
1 1/2 cup water

DIRECTIONS:

Chop shrimp into bite-size pieces. Scramble eggs & add milk, salt & pepper. Cut onion & basil into small parts. Add to scrambled eggs. Heat frying pan or omelette pan. Baste with butter. Pour 1/2 mixture into pan. Let firm slightly. Add shrimp then pour over the balance of egg mixture. When brown on the bottom, flip over to brown the other side. Serve. Bring Quinoa and water to a boil. Cover and simmer 10 to 15 minutes until the water is absorbed.

SERVING SUGGESTIONS:

Serve with English muffins.

Bruce Rumage
Pawley's Island Running Club
Pawley's Island, South Carolina

"After the Run"
Banana French Toast

I N G R E D I E N T S :

4 slices whole grain bread
1 egg
2 tblsp. banana-orange juice concentrate
2 tblsp. apple juice concentrate
1/2 small banana
1/4 cup non-fat dry milk
vegetable cooking spray

D I R E C T I O N S :

Combine ingredients with milk, throw in the blender, and process until smooth. Soak bread in the concentrated mix until they are wet. Spray non-stick skillet with vegetable spray. Cook bread until nicely browned. Makes four slices.

> *Jim Miccio*
> Milford Road Runners
> Parent's Place 5K Pacer
> Stratford, Connecticut

Eagle Kountry Breakfast Casserole

INGREDIENTS:

6 eggs
1/2 cup shredded cheddar cheese
1/2 cup shredded mozzarella cheese
1 tsp. dry mustard
1 tblsp. parsley flakes
1 tblsp. dried onion flakes
1 tsp. oregano
1 lb. ground Italian sausage
1 cup biscuit mix
2 cups milk

DIRECTIONS:

Brown sausage, crumble & drain. Beat eggs & milk together lightly. Add all ingredients together in a large bowl & mix together. Pour into lightly greased 9"x13" baking pan. Cover & refrigerate over night. Bake 1 hour at 350°.

Makes 8 Servings

SERVING SUGGESTIONS:

Serve with fresh fruit.

Peggy Rittenberry
Army ROTC Golden Eagle 10K Race
Cookville, Tennessee

Arizona Eggs

INGREDIENTS:

3 corn tortillas - cut into 2" strips
3 tblsp. fat free chicken broth
1/2 cup diced onion
1-14.5 oz. can original style stewed tomatoes
1 cup shredded cooked turkey
1/2 cup green pepper strips
6 Egg Beaters - about 1 1/2 cups
1 cup grated non-fat mozzarella cheese or jack cheese

DIRECTIONS:

In a large skillet cook the tortillas in the chicken broth until golden. Remove & set aside. Add onion, cook until tender. Drain tomatoes reserving liquid. Add liquid to skillet. Cover & heat on high for 3 minutes. Stir occasionally. Stir in tomatoes, turkey & pepper. Heat through & reduce heat to low. Add tortillas & egg beaters. Cover & cook 4-6 minutes or until Egg Beaters are set. Sprinkle with cheese. Cover & heat 1 more minutes or until cheese is melted. Serve immediately.

SERVING SUGGESTIONS:

Serve on fiestaware dinner plate with a slice of either cantaloupe or watermelon or both. Also looks lovely with a small bunch of grapes off on the side.

> *Harvey Beller*
> New Times Phoenix 10K
> Phoenix, Arizona

Oatmeal Crunch

INGREDIENTS:

1/2 cup slow cook oatmeal(5 minute not Quick Oats)
2 tblsp. of Miller bran
1 tblsp. of brown sugar
1 cup water
milk
Granola or Shredded Wheat

DIRECTIONS:

Mix oatmeal, brown sugar, bran & water in microwave safe bowl. Cook for 3 1/2 minutes in microwave. Stir and let oatmeal stand for 2 minutes. Add milk to your preference for consistency. Add 1/2 cup of crunch cereal for "the crunch".

Serves 1

Jerome H. Loy
Track & Cross Country Jefferson Forest H.S., Coach
Goode, Virginia

Belgium Waffles

INGREDIENTS:

2-3 cups sifted flour
1 tsp. salt
1 tsp. baking soda
1 tsp. baking powder
1 tsp. vanilla
3 tblsp. oil
2 eggs
1 tsp. cinnamon
1/2 to 1 cup of milk

DIRECTIONS:

Sift 2 cups flour (or 3 if your feeding more). Combine dry ingredients while heating waffle iron. Fluff eggs with fork until frothy. Blend oil, vanilla & egg mixture & stir. Begin by putting 1/2 cup of milk & add more until it forms a nice consistency.

SERVING SUGGESTIONS:

Try it as a dessert by adding vanilla ice cream, strawberries & whipped topping with a cherry.

Linda Richards
Great Pumpkin Foot Race & Bradley Bulldog Fun Run
Bradley, California

Cantina Eggs

INGREDIENTS:

8 lrg. eggs
1/4 cup milk
1/2 green pepper
4 slices Velveeta cheese
1 can pork & beans
4 med. mushrooms
1 jalapeño pepper
1/4 red onion

DIRECTIONS:

Beat eggs in large mixing bowl. Blend in milk. Dice green pepper & add to bowl. Add cheese to bowl. Remove pork fat cube from pork & beans and add to bowl. Dice mushrooms & add to bowl. Dice jalapeño pepper, put in bowl. Dice red onion & add to bowl. Heat all ingredients in a large fry pan at 325°, stirring frequently until cheese is melted & eggs have a cooked fluffy texture. Top with picante sauce.

Makes 6-8 large portions.

SERVING SUGGESTIONS:

Serve with orange juice or V-8 juice & wheat toast. Best when eaten after a long morning run.

Robert Stickney
Medicine Lodge Lions Journey For Sight
Medicine Lodge, Kansas

Chicken and Spinach Quiche

INGREDIENTS:

4 boneless, skinless chicken breasts
2 lrg. eggs
2 cups shredded cheese (swiss, provolone, mozzarella, monterey jack)
1 sm. onion
1/4 cup skim milk
1 pkg. Stouffers Spinach Souffle
1 deep dish pie crust

DIRECTIONS:

Cut up chicken breasts & cook. Cook spinach souffle according to directions on package. In large bowl, add eggs, milk and mix. Stir in cheese, onion, cooked chicken & spinach. Pour into pie crust and cook at 325° for approximately 30-45 minutes.

SERVING SUGGESTIONS:

This recipe freezes well so make several at the same time so later you can just heat & serve. Serve with a fruit salad and wheat rolls.

Jane R. Alred
Gate River Run
Jacksonville, Florida

Monster Cinnamon Rolls

INGREDIENTS:

Dough:
3/4 cup unsalted butter
1 cup milk
3/4 cup + 1 tsp. sugar
1 1/4 tsp. active dry yeast
1/2 cup warm water
5 lrg. eggs
8 1/2 - 9 1/2 all purpose flour
Filling:
5 cup firmly packed brown sugar
1 1/4 cup unsalted butter
3 tblsp. ground cinnamon

Frosting:
1/2 lb. softened cream cheese
1/4 cup whipping cream
1 tsp. vanilla extract
3-4 cups sifted confectioners sugar
*Optional Chocolate Frosting:
5 cups white sugar
1 1/2 cups butter
3 tblsp. Ghirardelli ground chocolate

DIRECTIONS:

For dough: Heat butter with milk, 3/4 cup sugar & salt in a small sauce pan until butter is melted. Set aside to cool. In a large mixing bowl sprinkle the yeast over warm water, add the remaining teaspoon sugar, stir, & set aside for 10 minutes until mixture is bubbly. Add the lukewarm milk mixture & the eggs and beat until well combined. Add the flour a cup at a time, stirring and using enough flour to form a stiff dough. Turn out on a floured board and knead dough until smooth and satiny, approximately 10 minutes (or place in the bowl of an electric mixer and knead dough for 5 minutes). Place dough in a very large buttered bowl, turn to butter the top & allow to rise. Cover loosely with a kitchen towel in a warm place until doubled in bulk, approximately 1 hour. Punch the dough down & roll out to a large rectangle, 24"x36". Now butter two 9"x13" baking dishes. For the filling, beat together brown sugar, butter & cinnamon until well combined. Spread evenly over the surface of the dough. Roll up length-wise & cut at 2" intervals to make 12 rolls. Place 6 rolls in each buttered dish. Cover loosely with a kitchen towel & allow to rise until double in bulk (about 1 hour). Preheat oven to 350° & bake rolls for 20-30 minutes, or until puffed & brown. Cool to room temperature on racks.

Frosting: Beat cream cheese, cream & vanilla until well combined. Add the confectioners sugar & beat until smooth & soft, not stiff. Frost rolls & serve immediately.

*Use optional chocolate frosting if you don't like cinnamon filling. Makes 12 large rolls!

Kenna Dunlay
Fort Collins Running Club
Wellington, Colorado

La Have Scones

INGREDIENTS:

1 1/2 cup whole wheat pastry flour + 1 3/4 cup white unbleached flour
            (or 3 3/4 cup of any flour)
2 tblsp. wheat bran
1/4 cup grated coconut or rolled oats
3 3/4 tsp. baking powder
3/4 tsp. salt
3/4 cup sugar or unrefined cane sugar
Liquid:
1 egg
1/2 cup canola oil
2 tblsp. maple syrup
1 tsp. vanilla
1/2 cup milk (soy, rice, or dairy)
1/2 cup chopped raisins (a little flour keeps then from sticking)

DIRECTIONS:

Mix dry ingredients in a bowl. Mix wet ingredients in a large bowl. Then fold dry ingredients into the liquid ingredients, mix until a stiff dough is formed. Put onto a floured counter, knead four times. Make scones by rolling chunks of dough into balls, whatever size you want. Place balls on a hot pizza stone or ungreased cookie sheet. Bake in a pre-heated oven at 375° for 18-20 minutes. Great served plain, or with butter, jam or peanut butter. It is preferable to use organic ingredients.

SERVING SUGGESTIONS:

The idea of this recipe comes from La Have Nova Scotia. After running in the annual Eastern Passage & Cow-Bay Carnival 1996 10K Road Race. We took a cable ferry to get to the La Have bakery, where we had scones much like this recipe.

Linda Usher
Central Mass Striders
Upton, Massachusetts

Gramma's Rice Pudding

INGREDIENTS:

2/3 cup uncooked instant rice
1/4 cup sugar
1/8 tsp. salt
1/4 tsp. nutmeg
2 1/2 cup skim milk
1 tsp. vanilla
1 egg yolk
2 tblsp. skim milk

DIRECTIONS:

In a medium saucepan combine 1st six ingredients. Stir & bring to a full rolling boil. Cook over low heat, but still boiling for 20 minutes. Stir constantly. Beat 1 egg yolk with 2 tablespoons milk. Very slowly add to hot rice, stirring very rapidly. Cool. Serve warm or cold. Can add raisins according to taste.

SERVING SUGGESTIONS:

Great for a Sunday brunch.

Paulette Schwartz
Bessemer Hometown Run
Bessemer, Michigan

Notes

Many Muffins

Many Muffins

Karin's Runners Muffins

Poppy Citrus Muffins

Morning Glory Muffins

Bran Muffins

Huffin Puffin Muffin Loaves

Brown Sugar Muffins

Buds Banana Muffins

Cathy's Energy Treats

Kirsling Energy Bars

Edison Energy Bar

Energy Bombs

Carbocrunchies

Karin's Runners Muffins

INGREDIENTS:

1 lrg. shredded carrot
1 lrg. shredded apple
1/2 cup oil
2 eggs
1/2 cup honey or sugar
2 tsp. vanilla
1/2 cup coconut
1/2 cup currants or raisins
3/4 cup whole wheat flour
1/2 cup oats
3 tblsp. wheat germ
1 tsp. baking soda
1/2 tsp. baking powder
1/8 tsp. nutmeg
3/4 tsp. cinnamon
1/4 tsp. salt

DIRECTIONS:

Shred the carrot & apple in the Cuisinart, then mix everything together in a bowl. Spoon into greased tins and bake in oven at 375° for 20 minutes.
* May add nuts, cranberries, etc.

SERVING SUGGESTIONS:

Serve with homemade jam or jelly. These muffins give runners the kind of energy boost that they need! I can even count on my children liking them.

Karin Kyte Romero
Southern Colorado Runners Club
Beulah, Colorado

Poppy Citrus Muffins

INGREDIENTS:

Non-stick Cooking Spay
2 egg whites
1 whole egg
3/4 cup non fat plain yogurt
3/4 cup sugar
1/4 tsp. salt
1/4 tsp. dried lemon peel (or 1 tsp freshly grated lemon peel)
1 tsp. freshly grated orange peel or 1/4 tsp. of dried
1/2 cup skim milk
1 2/3 cup flour
2 tsp. baking powder
1 tblsp. poppy seeds

DIRECTIONS:

Heat oven to 375°. Lightly coat 12 muffin tin with non stick spray. In a big bowl combine egg whites, 1 whole egg, yogurt and sugar. Beat on medium speed till sugar is dissolved or about 2 minutes. Add salt, peels and milk, then beat until combined. In a separate bowl combine flour, baking powder and poppy seeds. Beat dry ingredients into liquid until incorporated. Spoon batter into prepared muffin tin. Bake 20 minutes or until golden on top and firm to touch. Allow to cool for 10 or 15 minutes and remove from tin. When cool, mix 1/4 cup powdered sugar and 1 teaspoon lemon juice together to form thin glaze. Drizzle lightly over the tops of muffins, allow to dry and store in air tight container.

SERVING SUGGESTIONS:

Great low fat snack for anytime!

Judy Moir
Boulder Road Runners
Nederland, Colorado

Morning Glory Muffins

INGREDIENTS:

1/2 cup raisins
2 cups all purpose flour
1 cup sugar
2 tsp. baking soda
2 tsp. cinnamon
1/2 tsp. salt
2 cups grated peeled carrots

1 lrg. peeled, cored and grated tart green apple
1/2 cup sliced almonds
1/2 cup shredded coconut
3 eggs
2/3 cup vegetable oil
2 tsp. vanilla

DIRECTIONS:

Soak raisins in hot water to cover for 30 minutes. Drain thoroughly. Preheat oven to 375°. Line 24 muffin cups with baking cups. Mix dry ingredients in bowl. Stir in raisins, carrots, apple, almonds, and coconut. Beat eggs with oil and vanilla to blend. Stir into flour mixture until just combined. Divide among muffin cups. Bake until muffins are golden brown and tester in center comes out clean, 20-22 minutes. Cool 5 minutes. Remove from pan. Serve at room temperature.

Makes 2 dozen

SERVING SUGGESTIONS:

These muffins are a great crowd pleaser after a morning run. I often take them when we go out of town to a race with a group of friends. They are not low in fat, but are high in taste and great energy boosters. (Much more flavorful than power bars.)

Jane M.Nelson
Lady White Rose Run
York Road Runners Club
York, Pennsylvania

Bran Muffins

INGREDIENTS:

3 cups all purpose flour
2 cups whole wheat flour
2 1/2-3 cups sugar
5 cups raisin bran flakes
1 cup all-bran
1 cup chopped nuts
5 tsp. soda
4 eggs
1 qt. buttermilk
1 cup oil

DIRECTIONS:

Beat eggs thoroughly with electric mixer and then beat with other liquid ingredients. Mix the solid ingredients into the liquid. Let the batter stand 1 day in refrigerator and then use when desired (will keep up to six weeks). Bake in muffin pans for 20 minutes @ 400°.

Makes 48 muffins

> Jay R. Burns
> Owensboro Running/Walking Club
> Owensboro, Kentucky

Huffin' Puffin' Muffin Loaves

INGREDIENTS:

6 cups flour
2 pkgs. dry yeast
1 tsp. sugar
2 tsp. salt
1/4 tsp. baking soda
2 cup non-fat milk
1/2 cup water
cornmeal
vegetable spray

DIRECTIONS:

Combine 3 cups flour, yeast, sugar, salt & soda. Heat liquids until very warm (120°-130°F). Add to dry mixture. Beat well. Stir in remaining flour to make a stiff batter. Divide into two 8 1/2"x4 1/2" pans that have been sprayed with vegetable spray and sprinkled with cornmeal. Sprinkle tops of dough with cornmeal. Cover with plastic wrap. Let rise in warm place for 45 minutes or until doubled. Bake at 400° for 25 minutes or until lightly browned. Remove from pans immediately & cool.

SERVING SUGGESTIONS:

Slice, toast and spread with your favorite jam or jelly. This bread freezes well.

James Engel
Upper Peninsula Road Runners Club
Wakefield, Michigan

Brown Sugar Muffins

INGREDIENTS:

1 cup brown sugar
1/2 cup butter or margarine
1 egg
1 cup milk
2 cups flour
1 tsp. baking powder
1/2 tsp. soda
1/2 tsp. salt
1/2 tsp vanilla
1/2 cup chopped pecans

DIRECTIONS:

Cream butter and sugar. Add egg and milk, stir well to combine. Add dry ingredients, nuts and vanilla. Don't over-mix. Fill greased muffin pans 2/3 full. Bake at 425° for 12-15 minutes.

Susan Alexander
Mesa Monument Striders
Whitewater, Colorado

Bud's Banana Muffins

INGREDIENTS:

4 med. bananas whipped up well
2 tblsp. baking powder
2 eggs
1 tblsp. of vanilla
8 cups flour

DIRECTIONS:

Mix up bananas, baking powder, eggs and vanilla. Use non-fat cooking spray on tins for muffin pan. Pour or spoon ingredients into muffin form. Make sure you fill over top if you want huge muffin with huge tops.

Bud James
Park Forest Scenic 10 Mile Run
Homewood, Illinois

Cathy's Energy Treats

INGREDIENTS:

* Here's a new twist on a familiar favorite.

1 cup toasted and chopped pecan pieces
1/8 cup lightly toasted sesame seeds
1/8 cup flax seeds
1/2 cup lightly toasted sunflower seeds
1/2 cup dried chopped fruit: I like a combination of raisins and dried
    cranberries, but dried apricots are also very good
1/4 cup canola oil
12 oz. regular marshmallows (about 55)
7 cups combination of crispy rice, multi-grain flakes, and oat-Os cereal

DIRECTIONS:

Lightly toast nuts separately in toaster oven or dry skillet. Coarsely chop pecans. Mix all nuts and chopped fruit together. Combine dry cereal in a bowl. Add fruit-nut mixture to cereal. In a large pot, over low heat, heat the canola oil. (Using a spatula "pull" some of the oil up the sides of the pot. This will prevent the marshmallow mixture from sticking later on, making clean up easier.) Add the marshmallows and stir until completely melted. Add the cereal-fruit-nut mixture and stir well, making sure everything is well coated with the melted marshmallows. Using an oiled spatula, pour mixture into a 13"x9"x2" cake pan coated with cooking oil spray and press firmly. Let cool and cut into squares. Enjoy!

Catherine Pagani
Tuscaloosa Track Club
Tuscaloosa, Alabama

Kirsling Energy Bars

INGREDIENTS:

24 dried figs
1/3 cup honey
6 tblsp. orange juice concentrate,
   thawed
2 tblsp. lemon juice
1 cup whole wheat flour
1 cup corn flour
1/2 tsp. baking soda
1/4 tsp. baking powder

1 tblsp. canola oil
1/4 cup dark corn syrup
2 egg whites
1/2 cup raisins
3/4 cup oats, old fashioned
1/2 tsp. cinnamon
1/8 cup molasses
1/4 cup chopped toasted almonds
1/4 cup chocolate chips

DIRECTIONS:

Place figs, honey, orange juice concentrate, lemon juice into food processor & mix on chop setting until figs are finely cut. Set aside. Put all other ingredients in mixing bowl. Best with electric mixer for 3-4 minutes at medium speed. Add fig mixture & beat until everything blends. Spread into a 9"x13" pan sprayed with no stick spray. Bake @ 350° 25-30 minutes. Score top for lattice cutting. Place in refrigerator to harden. Cut at pre-scored areas. (Score for cutting of small squares.) Store in air tight container. They freeze well.

SERVING SUGGESTIONS:

Great before, after or during a run or bike ride! They pack well.

Kathy Kirsling
Albuquerque Road Runners Club
Albuquerque, New Mexico

"Edison" Energy Bars

INGREDIENTS:

2 tblsp. butter
2 cups miniature marshmallows
2 tblsp. peanut butter
4 cups high protein cereal

DIRECTIONS:

Melt butter or margarine in skillet @ 300°. Add marshmallows. Stir till mixture is melted and syrupy. Remove from heat. Stir in peanut butter. Add cereal and mix until coated. Press softly into 8"x8" pan with heavy foil on the bottom. Cool until firm. Cut into 2"x2" squares.

Makes 16 bars

SERVING SUGGESTIONS:

Great race day energy.

Charles J. Malone III
Edison Cross Country
Huron, Ohio

"Energy Bombs"

I N G R E D I E N T S :

1/2 cup Tupelo honey
1/2 cup crunchy peanut butter
1 cup non-fat dry milk
dry skim milk (prefer Jerrell's because it has a smooth consistency)
raisins (optional)
nuts (optional)
dried fruit (optional)

D I R E C T I O N S :

Place all ingredients into a bowl. Stir with a spoon until all the ingredients
are mixed together and form a ball. Knead the ball for about 2-3 minutes,
roll into a log shape, slice about 1/2 inch thick, roll each into mini logs.
Then roll each log into powdered sugar. Can be stored in plastic bags for
easy access. *These are the poor mans energy bars. They come in handy
around the 10 mile mark of a trail run or after about after 1 1/2 hours of vigorous exercise (like mountain biking).

S E R V I N G   S U G G E S T I O N S :

If you are short on time & patience, just roll the log, put the whole thing in
the freezer and slice a portion when you need it or when you just want a
quick snack that is power packed. Happy Trails!!

Meshelle Pate
Huntsville Track Club
Huntsville, Alabama

Carbocrunchies

INGREDIENTS:

1 cup sugar
1 cup white corn syrup
1/2 tsp. salt
1/2 tsp. vanilla
1 cup peanut butter
8 cups corn flakes

DIRECTIONS:

Mix together the sugar and syrup in a pan, and bring to a boil. Add salt, vanilla, peanut butter and corn flakes. Mix gently without crushing. Drop by spoonfuls on wax paper. Cool. Makes about 50.

Joel Allred
Cache Sun and Snow Runners
Hyde Park, Utah

Hot & Cold Running Pasta

Hot & Cold Running Pasta

Pineywoods Pacers Power Noodle Casserole

Paul Perry Pre Race Pasta Dinner

Italian Marathon Pasta Salad

Sunny Pasta Salad

Lovers Leap Lasagna

Rob's Penne with Eggplant and Chicken

Duffy's Favorite

Gary's Vegetable Lasagna

Theresa's Terrific Ziti

Pasta with Flair

Low-Fat Chicken Pasta Alfredo

Barb's Spaghetti and Meatballs

Linguine with Chicken

Spinach Yogurt Lasagna

Primo Veggie Pasta

Carol's Chicky Spaghetti

Noodles Excellanté

Zippy Lemon-Basil Pasta

Greek Pasta

"Trolley Run" Artichoke Pasta Energizer

Peanut Pork Lo Mein

Vegetarian Lasagna

Mediterranean Chicken Pasta

P.R. Pasta

First Marathon Pasta Salad

Pineywoods Pacers
Power Noodle Casserole

INGREDIENTS:

1 lb. ground beef, chicken or turkey
1 can Ranch Style beans
1 can Ro-tel tomatoes
1 can low fat mushroom or chicken soup
1/4 cup chopped onion
6 oz pkg. cooked egg noodles
garlic powder (optional)
grated fat free cheese for topping (optional)

DIRECTIONS:

Brown ground meat with chopped onion; add garlic powder. Drain meat, add beans, Ro-tel tomatoes, soup & cooked egg noodles. Place in casserole dish; top with grated cheese if desired. Bake @ 350° approximately. 30 minutes.

SERVING SUGGESTIONS:

Great with baked tortilla chips and salsa!

Debby Duren
Pineywoods Pacers Running Club
Lufkin, Texas

Paul Perry
Pre-Race Pasta Dinner

INGREDIENTS:

2 lb. boneless chicken breast-pound and slice into strips
2 pkgs. sliced portabello mushrooms
1 lrg. diced zucchini
1 1/2 boxes ziti with lines
2 lrg. chopped tomatoes
chopped fresh basil
6 cloves chopped fresh garlic
lemon pepper
onion powder
paprika
1 tblsp. lemon juice
1/4 cup white wine
2 chicken bouillon cubes - dissolved in 1 1/2 cups of water

DIRECTIONS:

Sprinkle chicken with lemon pepper & paprika. Sprinkle mushrooms with a little olive oil. Grill chicken and mushrooms and set aside. Sauté basil & garlic in 3 tablespoons olive oil. Add tomatoes, zucchini. Sauté until tender. Add liquid bouillon, lemon juice, white wine & about 1/4 teaspoon each of lemon pepper & onion powder. Add grilled chicken & mushrooms. Cover & simmer on low heat. Boil pasta until done. Drain and toss with 2 tablespoons olive oil. Combine chicken mixture with pasta. Toss and serve.

Serves 6 HARDY appetites!

SERVING SUGGESTIONS:

Sprinkle freshly grated parmesan cheese on top. Goes great with white wine and Italian bread.

> *Mary Ellen Borge*
> The Paul Perry 5 Mile Road Race
> Glouchester, Massachusetts

Italian Marathon Pasta Salad

INGREDIENTS:

Salad:
6 oz. (2 1/2 cups) rotini macaroni salad
1 tblsp. butter
2 cups broccoli florets & stems cut into pieces the size of a quarter
1 1/2 cups tomato cut in chunks the size of quarter
1 cup red, green, or yellow bell pepper cut in to pieces the size of a nickel
1/2 sm. onion (1/2 cup) peeled and sliced with the rings separated

1 can (2 1/4 oz.) black olives, sliced and strained
6 oz. pepperoni or 9 oz. diced ham (optional)
lettuce leaves

Dressing:
3 tblsp. olive oil
1/4 cup fresh parsley cut fine
2 tblsp. vinegar
1 tsp. garlic salt

DIRECTIONS:

Steps that are done ahead of baking:
Cook the pasta & broccoli. The morning or night before you serve the salad, cook the pasta as directed on the package. Drain it; stir in the butter; cover and refrigerate. Cut the broccoli and discard the woody stems. Bring 3 quarts of water to a boil and add the broccoli. After it comes back to a boil, cook for 2 minutes. Run it under cold water, drain cover and refrigerate.
Cooking:
When the broccoli and pasta are cold, prepare the other vegetables. Mix and serve. In a large salad bowl, whisk together the oil, parsley, vinegar, & salt. Add the vegetables; broccoli, tomato, bell pepper, onion, & olives. Add the pasta and if using, add pepperoni or ham. Stir. Refrigerate.

SERVING SUGGESTIONS:

Serve on a piece of lettuce with a pickle, toast & butter, bagel & cream cheese, or a fried egg sandwich. With this recipe, the salad dressing is barley noticeable, and the calories from the fat are few. The dressing is clear and not creamy.

Yield; 10 cups or 5 servings.

Mark Sohn
Indiana Road Runners Club
Indiana, Pennsylvania

Sunny Pasta Salad

I N G R E D I E N T S :

12 oz. pkg. spiral pasta
1/2 cup chopped sundried tomatoes
1 lrg. red bell pepper
1 tblsp. olive oil
2 tsp. minced fresh garlic
1/3 cup pine nuts (pignolias)
1/3 cup shredded parmesan cheese
1 1/4 cup Italian salad dressing
3 tblsp. balsamic vinegar
1/4 cup chopped fresh basil (optional)
1/2 cup marinated artichoke hearts (optional)

D I R E C T I O N S :

Cook pasta according to package directions. Cool. Brown pine nuts in olive oil, stirring frequently to prevent scorching. Add garlic after 3 minutes. Cook together until nuts are lightly browned. Set aside to cool. Add dried tomatoes, peppers, parmesan, dressing, vinegar, basil and artichoke hearts to pasta. Add cooled garlic & pine nuts. Toss. Refrigerate & allow flavors to blend for 1-2 hours before serving. Garnish top with parmesan & a few basil leaves.

Hugh Snook/Steve Tronnes
Strawberry Striders Running Club
John Day, Oregon

Lover's Leap Lasagna

INGREDIENTS:

1 lb. ground beef	1 container cottage cheese (sm.)
1/4 cup chopped onion	1/4 cup parmesan cheese
1/2 tsp. minced garlic	1 tblsp. parsley
1/2 tsp. salt	1/4 tsp. pepper
1/2 tsp. pepper	2 beaten eggs
1 can tomato sauce (sm.)	8 pieces lasagna
1 can tomato paste (sm.)	2 cups shredded mozzarella
1 can canned tomatoes	

DIRECTIONS:

Brown ground beef, drain grease and crumble. Stir in next 7 ingredients. Microwave 5 minutes. Stir. Microwave 5 more minutes. Preheat oven to 375° (for premade refrigerated lasagna), 350° for freshly made lasagna. In the meantime, start lasagna noodles (cook according to directions). Mix together; eggs, cottage cheese, parmesan cheese, parsley & pepper. Layer in 9"x13" dish. Noodles, cheese mixtures, mozzarella, ground beef mixture. Repeat. Top ground beef mixture with 1/4 cup parmesan cheese. Bake 55 minutes @ 350°.

SERVING SUGGESTIONS:

Fast, fun & full of carbos!!! Lover's Leap Lasagna will have your guests "leaping for more!" Freezes well and saves you time for more training in the "Hannibal Cannibal" which takes you to Lover's Leap in Hannibal, MO.

Marisa Brown
Hannibal Cannibal
Hannibal, Missouri

Rob's Penne with Eggplant and Chicken

INGREDIENTS:

1 lb. Penne (Quill shaped) pasta
4 tblsp. olive oil
1 med.-lrg. eggplant, peeled and cut into 1" cubes
4 cloves finely chopped garlic
35 oz. can drained and finely chopped Italian tomatoes
1/4 tsp. dried hot pepper flakes
1/2 tsp. salt
1 1/2 tblsp. chopped parsley
1/2 to 1 lb. cooked chicken cut into strips or cubes
freshly ground pepper (to taste)
grated parmesan cheese

DIRECTIONS:

Bring a large pot of salted water to boil. Add the pasta and cook until tender but slightly firm. When you start the water, begin the sauce. In a large skillet heat 2 tablespoon oil over medium high heat until hot but not smoking. Add 1/2 the eggplant and cook, tossing frequently until almost tender. Transfer to a heated plate. Add another tablespoon oil and repeat with remaining eggplant, and add to the plate.

Add the remaining tablespoon of oil to the skillet and sauté until pale gold, about 1 minute. Add tomatoes, red pepper flakes, chicken & salt, pepper to taste. Add the eggplant and cook until sauce is thickened and the eggplant is tender. Takes approximately 10-15 minutes. Keep the sauce hot if the pasta is not done yet. Drain pasta in a colander. Place in warm serving bowl and add sauce. Toss well, add the parsley and toss again.

SERVING SUGGESTIONS:

Serve with a bowl of grated parmesan cheese. Good with salad and French bread.

Marietjie Quicke
AORTA - Auburn Opelika Road & Track Association
Aurburn, Alabama

Duffy's Favorite

INGREDIENTS:

2 cups carrots
1 cup green onion
2 cups zucchini
2 cucumbers
2 cups peppers
2 cloves garlic
2 tblsp. olive oil
3-4 tblsp. Ketjap Manis (Conimex) - (sweet soy sauce)
1 or 2 pkgs. Angel Hair Pasta
3 cups grated cheese
3-4 lbs. diced chicken breast
water chestnuts, bean sprouts (optional)

DIRECTIONS:

Thinly slice carrots, onions, zucchini, cucumbers, peppers, & minced garlic. Preheat wok or large skillet, add oil, onions, garlic. Then add diced chicken. Cook until chicken is done. Add one cup water then add sliced vegetables, cover and stir often. Cook until vegetables are tender. Cook pasta per directions on the package. When vegetables are done add Ketjap Manis, stir and serve.

SERVING SUGGESTIONS:

Serve over pasta with grated cheese as a topping. If you are serving vegetarians leave out the chicken. More Ketjap Manis may be added at serving time.

Cathy Groos
Goose Creek Run Off
Kaysville, Utah

Gary's Vegetable Lasagna

INGREDIENTS:

4 spinach sheets (preferably fresh)*
4 tomato/herb sheets
3 lbs. low fat Ricotta cheese
2 eggs
2 cups each of diced broccoli, zucchini, squash, tomatoes, peppers (green or red)
2 jars marinara
2 cups mozzarella cheese
*Sheets are lasagna noodles

DIRECTIONS:

Spray 9 1/2"x11" pan. In bowl mix eggs, skim milk, fresh garlic, seasonings & ricotta cheese (the marinara sauce will thin the sauce out later). Thicken with mozzarella. Fold in diced vegetables. Begin building in the 9 1/2"x11" pan. Lay out 1 sheet spinach sheet & spread a thin layer of marinara sauce. Add enough vegetable mixture to cover sufficiently. Continue to do the last step alternating layers in the same fashion. Top with mozzarella and bake @ 400° for 50 minutes.

SERVING SUGGESTIONS:

Top with marinara & fresh parmesan cheese when serving. Great with garlic bread. A signature dish at Gary's Surf Spray Cafe, health food restaurant in Dewey Beach, Delaware.

Ava Seaney Cannon
Dewey Beach Sprint Triathlon
Rehoboth, Delaware

Theresa's Terrific Ziti

INGREDIENTS:

1 lb. box ziti noodles
2-28 oz. jars spaghetti sauce
1 cup grated Parmesan cheese
3 cups grated mozzarella cheese

DIRECTIONS:

Cook ziti noodles according to package directions. Drain and mix 1 1/2 jars pasta sauce with drained noodles. Mix to coat noodles. Put 1/2 of the noodle mixture into 13"x9" casserole dish. Sprinkle on 1/2 cup grated Parmesan cheese and 1 1/2 cups grated mozzarella cheese. Repeat layers with remaining noodles and cheeses. Top with remaining pasta sauce. Bake @ 350° for 30-40 minutes until hot and bubbly. Let cook a few minutes before serving.

Serves 8-10

SERVING SUGGESTIONS:

All that is needed to complete this meal is a tossed green salad and some baked bread and iced tea or milk. A fruit cup of cantaloupe, honeydew melon, and blueberries is a good dessert or you can't go wrong with a dish of low-fat ice cream.

Jack Marshell Toms
Lynchburg College Cross Country & Track
Forest, Virginia

Pasta With Flair

INGREDIENTS:

1/2 cup olive oil
2 cloves minced garlic
2 oz. tin of anchovies
3.5 oz. jar of capers
1 lb. spinach - steamed & drained
1/2 cup fresh grated parmesan
Pasta for four - your choice - I like spirals (rotini)

DIRECTIONS:

Start pasta water to boil, add pasta when boiling. While water is heating, sauté garlic in olive oil - do not burn. Add anchovies chopped and mashed to the oil (on medium heat). Add drained capers chopped and mashed to the oil. Steam spinach, drain, chop and add to the oil. When pasta is cooked, drain, add olive oil sauce, add cheese mix in.

SERVING SUGGESTIONS:

Serve with more cheese on the side. Crusty bread, salad, maybe some wine and you have a quick, delicious meal.

Dr. Les Rosenbloom
Red Baron Half-Marathon
Painted Post, New York

Low-fat Chicken Pasta Al Fredo

INGREDIENTS:

6 1/2 cups med. shells, uncooked
1/4 cup margarine
2-5 minced garlic cloves
1 1/2 cups skim milk
1 tblsp cornstarch
1/3 cup grated parmesan cheese
2 lbs. julienne chicken breast
1/3 cup freshly chopped basil
1/4 tsp. ground black pepper
parmesan cheese - as needed

DIRECTIONS:

Cook pasta according to package directions, drain. Meanwhile in sauce pan over medium heat, melt margarine. Add garlic, cook until tender and brown. In small cup stir together 1 tablespoon milk and cornstarch. Add remaining milk to saucepan, stir in cornstarch mixture and cheese. Cook, stirring frequently, until sauce is slightly thickened. Stir in chicken, basil and pepper. Season with salt if desired. Serve over hot pasta. Add more parmesan cheese if desired.

Makes 8 - 4 oz. servings

SERVING SUGGESTIONS:

Serve over hot pasta. If desired add more parmesan cheese.

Dave Salmon
Lancaster Road Runners Club
Elizabethtown, Pennsylvania

Barb's Spaghetti and Meatballs

INGREDIENTS:

Meatballs;
1 lb. ground beef
1/4 lb. Italian sausage (loose)
2/3 cups bread crumbs
1/3 cup grated parmesan cheese
dash salt & pepper
Garlic salt - added until you can smell the garlic
1-2 eggs
add enough milk to make moist
Sauce;
1 can lrg. tomato sauce
1 can lrg. tomato paste
1/2-3/4 tsp. sweet basil & enough garlic salt to smell
1/2 tsp. salt
1/2 tsp. pepper

DIRECTIONS:

Mix all ingredients together. Separate into individual meatballs. Brown in oil. Then place in tomato sauce as it cooks. (If the meat is fatty you may have to skim off the top of sauce).

SERVING SUGGESTIONS:

The key to this recipe is the sausage and bread crumbs in the meatballs and the simmering of the sauce with the meatballs in it. The flavor that the sauce picks up from the meatballs is out of this world. Use whatever type of pasta noodles you like. This is my mom's recipe & my absolute favorite!

Benjamin J. Paulillo
Purdue Track Club
West Lafayette, Indiana

Linguine With Chicken

INGREDIENTS:

1 1/2 cup green pepper chopped into 1" pieces
1 1/2 cup red sweet pepper chopped into 1" pieces
1 cup onion sliced into 1" pieces
16 oz. Linguine or Penne pasta - uncooked
1 lb. cooked boneless chicken breast- cut into 1" pieces
1/4 cup teriyaki glaze sauce
1/4 cup dark sesame oil
1/2 oil chopped fresh parsley
2 tsp. chopped fresh thyme (or dried thyme)
salt/fresh ground pepper to taste
2 med. tomatoes, cut into wedges

DIRECTIONS:

In microwave safe bowl, stir together peppers & onion, microwave at high (100%) 2-3 minutes or until crisp tender. Rinse in cold water. Cook pasta according to package directions. Drain. Rinse with cold water to cool quickly. Drain well. In large bowl toss cooled pasta, vegetables and all remaining ingredients except tomatoes. Cover and refrigerate 1 hour. Serve at room temperature. Before serving, perk up flavors by tossing and adding a little bit of teriyaki glaze. Garnish with tomato wedges and additional parsley and thyme.

Makes 12 -1 1/2 cup servings

SERVING SUGGESTIONS:

Let stand at room temperature for 1 hour, re-toss ingredients adding just a touch of teriyaki glaze while tossing. Use large, flat pasta dish and place contents on dish. Garnish with tomato wedges and thyme parsley. Sprinkle fresh ground pepper & salt to taste. Serve on flat plate with warm baguettes sliced diagonal. (Parmesan cheese is optional)

Kevin Gallerani
Mohegan Striders
Uncasville, Connecticut

Spinach Yogurt Lasagna

INGREDIENTS:

2-10 oz. pkgs frozen chopped spinach
24 oz. cottage cheese
2 eggs, slightly beaten
3/4 cup parmesan cheese
1 tsp salt
1/2 tsp paprika
1/3 cup bread or cracker crumbs
9 lasagna noodles, cooked
1/4 cup butter or margarine
1/2 cup sliced mushrooms
1/2 cup chopped onions
6 tsp. flour
1/2 cup milk
2 cups yogurt

DIRECTIONS:

Steam spinach and drain very well. Mix the next six ingredients. Sauté mushrooms & onions in butter. Add yogurt & milk, stir for one minute, then add enough flour to thicken the mixture. Make 3 layers in a 9"x13" baking dish with the following proportions; 3 lasagna noodles topped with 1/3 spinach mixture. This is delicious!

Serves 6 hungry people

> *Susan Hamilton*
> Mountain Triathlon
> McCall, Idaho

Primo Veggie Pasta

INGREDIENTS:

1 med. zucchini peeled
1 med. yellow squash
1/2 cup or more onion
1 med. green pepper
1 bunch broccoli
1 sm. cauliflower
3 carrots
3 tblsp. olive oil
4 cloves fresh garlic
2 tsp. oregano
1 tsp. basil
1 tsp. parsley
pepper to taste
16 oz. (or more) canned marinara sauce
optional: 1 can garbanzo beans

DIRECTIONS:

Chop veggies into bite size pieces or a little bigger. Sauté garlic in olive oil. Stir in and sauté broccoli, cauliflower, carrots, and spices. Add the rest of the veggies. While the vegetables are still slightly crunchy, add marinara sauce, cook until heated thoroughly. Do not over cook, as veggies can become too mushy.

SERVING SUGGESTIONS:

Serve over vermicelli, angel hair or any other favorite pasta.

Janet Foster
River to River Runners
Metropolis, Illinois

Carol's Chicky Spaghetti

INGREDIENTS:

1 lb. thin spaghetti
1 boiled chicken
4 finely chopped, celery sticks
1 sm. finely chopped, green pepper
1 sm. finely chopped, onion
2-16 oz. cans stewed tomatoes
1 can cream of mushroom soup
1 can golden mushroom soup
1 lb. shredded mild cheddar cheese

DIRECTIONS:

Boil chicken and vegetables. Keep some broth. Remove meat from the bones & add tomatoes, soups & vegetables. Mix with boiled spaghetti, add some of the broth for moisture. Spread cheese over top, cover and bake @ 350° for 45 minutes.

SERVING SUGGESTIONS:

Garlic bread and salad complete the meal.

> *Carol Schreiber*
> Stagecoach Festival 5K
> New Lebanon, Ohio

Noodles Excellante

INGREDIENTS:

8 oz. dried rice noodles
4 sliced mushrooms
4 oz. broccoli florets
1 finely sliced carrot
8 oz asparagus, cut into 2" pieces
1 red or yellow seeded, and sliced pepper
2 oz. sugar snap peas
1 tblsp. olive oil
2 chopped garlic cloves
2 chopped green onions
1 lb. chopped tomatoes
1 tblsp. freshly chopped ginger
1 tblsp. soy sauce
black pepper & salt

DIRECTIONS:

Soak noodles in hot water for 30 minutes until soft, drain. Blanch broccoli, sliced carrots, asparagus, snap peas, separately in boiling salted water. Drain, rinse under cold water and drain again. Set aside. Heat olive oil in frying pan. Add ginger, garlic, onion and mushrooms. Stir fry for 30 seconds, then add tomatoes and stir fry 2-3 minutes. Add noodles and stir fry for 3 minutes. Toss in blanched vegetables. Season with soy sauce, salt, pepper and cook until vegetables are tender.

Serves 8

SERVING SUGGESTIONS:

Other vegetables may be substituted to give the dish variety and to suit different tastes.

Larry J. Richardson
Derby Running Club
Derby, Kansas

Zippy Lemon-Basil Pasta

INGREDIENTS:

1 cup dried bow tie pasta (about 3 oz.)
1 1/2 cups loose-pack frozen broccoli, green beans, pearl onions & red,
    sweet peppers mixture
3 tblsp. margarine
1 tblsp. snipped fresh parsley
2 tsp. snipped fresh basil
1 tsp. finely shredded lemon peel
3 tblsp. lemon juice
1 clove garlic (minced)
dash ground red pepper
1/8 tsp. salt

DIRECTIONS:

Cook pasta 8-10 minutes or till tender, adding frozen vegetables for last 5 minutes of cooking time. Drain well. Meanwhile, in a small saucepan melt margarine. Stir in parsley, basil, lemon peel, lemon juice, garlic, ground red pepper, and salt. Pour over pasta and vegetable mixture; toss gently to coat.

Serves 4

SERVING SUGGESTIONS:

If you are a light eater this is the perfect meal with a piece of garlic toast. Also makes a great side dish.

Krist A. Heid
Waco Striders
Clifton, Texas

Greek Pasta

INGREDIENTS:

1 lb. cooked farfalle pasta (save 1 1/2 cup pasta water)
1/2 cup coarsely chopped greek olives
3 garlic cloves (minced)
8 oz. crumbled feta
1 pkg. sundried tomatoes (not in oil) (chopped)
2 springs freshly chopped dill
1 1/2 cup chicken broth
2 tsp. olive oil

DIRECTIONS:

While pasta cooks, sauté garlic in oil, when light brown add olives, tomatoes & chicken broth. Simmer till tomatoes are soft. When pasta is cooked, drain pasta and add 1/2 cup pasta water to broth mixture. Put in serving bowl and sprinkle with cheese & dill. Serve.

SERVING SUGGESTIONS:

This tastes good as is, or with cooked chicken or shrimp.

Jeanette Nichols
Crosswicks, New Jersey

Trolley Run
Artichoke Pasta Energizer

INGREDIENTS:

8 oz. penne pasta (or choice)
1-15 oz. can artichoke hearts
2 minced cloves garlic
1 minced shallot (optional)
1/4 cup finely chopped onion
1/4 cup extra virgin olive oil
Fresh grated parmesan cheese

DIRECTIONS:

Drain artichokes. Cut off and discard tough leaves. Chop coarsely. Sauté onions, garlic and shallot in olive oil over medium-low heat until softened & cooked through. Add artichokes & heat. Meanwhile cook pasta according to directions or till cooked al dente. Drain. Toss with artichoke mixture.

SERVING SUGGESTIONS:

Artichoke pasta, tossed salad & hot Italian or sour dough bread. Have a small pitcher of extra virgin olive oil on the table to be served with the bread.

Judy Miller
Michael Forbes Trolley Run
Kansas City, Missouri

Peanut Pork Lo Mein

INGREDIENTS:

8 oz. spaghetti
2 cups frozen oriental vegetables
3/4 cup chicken broth
1/3 cup peanut butter
1 tblsp. soy sauce
1 tsp. curry powder
2 cups shredded or cubed pork (1 or 2 boneless chops)
2 cloves chopped garlic
1/4 tsp. cayenne pepper (optional)

DIRECTIONS:

Cook spaghetti according to directions. Meanwhile cook pork and garlic in small amount of oil. In a separate pan heat vegetables in chicken broth. Add peanut butter, soy sauce and curry powder & pepper. Stir until peanut butter melts. Add pork and garlic and heat for 2 minutes (slightly thickened). Toss with hot, drained spaghetti.

Serves 2

SERVING SUGGESTIONS:

Serve with broccoli stir fry. Stir fry broccoli florets, chopped garlic, & pine nuts in a little oil until broccoli is crisp tender.

Neil Wilson
Tri-Cities Road Runners
Colonial Heights, Virginia

Vegetarian Lasagna

INGREDIENTS:

Sauce:
2-1 lb. cans chopped tomatoes with juice
2 to 3 chopped stalks celery
1 med. chopped onion
3 to 4 chopped zucchini(sm.)
1/2 tsp. minced garlic
1 tblsp. chopped parsley
1/4 tsp. black pepper
1 tsp. ground oregano
12 oz. can tomato paste
Cheese Mixture:
1 lb. low fat mozzarella cheese
3/4 lb. low fat Ricotta or cottage cheese
1/4 cup Egg Beaters
2 tblsp. grated Parmesan cheese
2 tblsp. chopped parsley
1/8 tsp. pepper

DIRECTIONS:

Combine all of the sauce ingredients in a saucepan. Simmer 3/4 to 1 hour. Cook 1/2 lb lasagna noodles according to package directions. Next, mix Ricotta cheese together with next four items in bowl. Arrange in layers in 9"x13" baking dish sprayed with Pam as follows: sauce, noodles, Ricotta cheese mixture, mozzarella cheese; repeat. Sprinkle with 1/4 cup grated Parmesan cheese. Bake @ 350° for 3/4 to 1 hour or until mozzarella cheese is melted and all is hot throughout. Let sit 10 to 15 minutes before cutting. Can be made ahead of time and refrigerated before baking - allow a little longer for cooking.

Dee Crowe
BBC Striders
Belleville, Michigan

Mediterranean Chicken Pasta

INGREDIENTS:

1 cup extra virgin olive oil
4 tblsp. low-fat butter or margarine
1 lb. boneless, skinless chicken breasts
1/2 cup balsamic vinegar
1 bunch chopped green onions
1-8 oz. pkg or fresh sliced mushrooms
3 fresh Italian Plum Tomatoes chopped and seeded
1/4 cup drained capers
1 lb. angel hair pasta, prepared according to directions

DIRECTIONS:

Heat olive oil and butter in a large sauté pan and sauté chicken on high heat until brown. Remove chicken from pan and set aside. Lower heat and deglaze pan with vinegar and let sizzle for 1 minute. Add onions & mushrooms and sauté lightly. If desired, shred chicken, return it to pan with onions & mushrooms. Stir thoroughly and add tomatoes & capers, stirring till lightly cooked. Serve over angel hair pasta.

Serves 4-6

Kathleen Callaghan
Club South Runners
Baton Rouge, Louisiana

P.R. Pasta

INGREDIENTS:

2 chicken breasts skinned and deboned
1 cup chicken broth
1/2 cup orange juice
1/3 cup peach preserves
3 tblsp. chopped onions
1/8 tsp. ginger
1/2 cup half & half
1 each sm. red, yellow & orange peppers
2 tsp. tarragon
1 lb. fettuccini
1/3 cup mozzarella cheese
1/4 cup parmesan cheese
cracked black pepper

DIRECTIONS:

In a heavy skillet with a lid, steam cubed chicken breasts in chicken broth, orange juice & onions. When the chicken is cooked add ginger, preserves, half & half & tarragon. Simmer over medium heat for about 15 minutes. While chicken mixture is simmering, prepare fettuccini according to directions. Add the two cheeses & peppers to the chicken mixture. Cook for about 4 minutes or until the peppers are tender and the cheese begins to melt. Toss prepared noodles & chicken mixture. Season with cracked pepper.

SERVING SUGGESTIONS:

This colorful pasta makes the perfect pre-race dinner with a quick preparation, you can spend your tapering time with focusing on your strategy for a race. P.R. rather than slaving in the kitchen.

> *Laurie Nakauchi-Hawn*
> Colorado Columbines Women's Running Club
> Arvada, Colorado

First Marathon Pasta Salad

INGREDIENTS:

12 oz. pkg. Orzo pasta (long grain style, not round)
4 oz. pkg. wild rice
1 green pepper
1 red or yellow pepper
1 bunch green onions
1/2 cup chopped or sliced black olives
1/2 cup chopped or sliced green olives
16 oz. bottle Italian salad dressing (I recommend Paul Newman's)
8 oz. feta cheese
1/2 cup halved cherry tomatoes

DIRECTIONS:

While cooking Orzo & wild rice according to package instructions, chop peppers & onions. Make pieces small enough to be consistent with pasta, but big enough to crunch. Combine cooled pasta & rice with vegetables, olives & salad dressing. Crumble feta cheese on top when ready to serve. Garnish with cherry tomatoes.

SERVING SUGGESTIONS:

Serve this in a clear glass bowl, or spoon onto lettuce leaves if serving individually. Use this recipe only as a basis for your own personal tastes. Substitute any vegetables that can be chopped.

Catherine Yoe Sadowski
Colonial Road Runners
Williamsburg, Virginia

Notes

Appeteasers

Appeteasers

Voo Doo Salsa

Mad Anthony Wayne Marinated Mushrooms

Goat's Breath

Chicken Curry Tartlets

Trail Food Pizza Snacks

Sawtooth Salsa

Heartbreak Hummus

Kooks

Spinach Roll-Ups

Middle Eastern Tabouli

Feta Stuffed Pasta Shells

Croatian Burek

Voo Doo Salsa

INGREDIENTS:

8 lrg. Roma tomatoes
1 yellow bell pepper
1/4 cup Bermuda onion
2 limes
3-5 jalapeño peppers
3 tblsp. fresh basil
1-8 oz. can crushed pineapple

DIRECTIONS:

Coarsely chop tomatoes, bell pepper and onion. Mix together with the juice from the limes. Mince and seed jalapeños (3 mild, 5 for hot) and finely chop basil. Add to the mixture. Thoroughly drain pineapple and add to salsa. Refrigerate at least 3 hours.

SERVING SUGGESTIONS:

Serve with corn chips as a refreshing change to ordinary salsa. This is great over grilled fish or chicken.

Wayne Bennett
Albuquerque Roadrunners Club
Albuquerque, New Mexico

Mad Anthony Wayne Marinated Mushrooms

INGREDIENTS:

1-8 oz. or more fresh mushrooms
1-2 cloves minced garlic
1/2 cup white vinegar
1/2 cup burgundy wine
1 cup olive oil
1/4 tsp. ground pepper
1 tsp. oregano
1/4 tsp. thyme
1/2 tsp. salt (optional)
1 bay leaf

DIRECTIONS:

Remove stems from mushrooms, wash caps and dry on towel. Combine all ingredients except bay leaf to create marinade. Place bay leaf in bottom of a jar or other sealable container. Add mushroom caps to container. Pour marinade over the caps. Seal container, then let container remain at room temperature for 3 hours. Refrigerate after 3 hours. *For richer flavor substitute balsamic vinegar, cold-pressed olive oil, and fresh oregano and thyme.

SERVING SUGGESTIONS:

Serve as an appetizer or with a meal.

> *Mitch V. Harper*
> Fort Wayne Track Club
> Fort Wayne, Indiana

Goat's Breath

INGREDIENTS:

4 flour tortillas
2 lrg. pkgs. of cream cheese (can use low fat cream cheese)
1-4 cloves of fresh garlic (use according to desired amount of garlic)
3 tblsp. salsa
2-3 tsp. black olives (diced)

DIRECTIONS:

Keep cream cheese out until it reaches room temperature. Mash cream cheese, garlic, salsa together. Do by hand, with a fork. When mixed well, fold in olives just until blended. Evenly distribute cheese mixture over entire tortillas. Don't skimp, spread generously. Roll up each tortilla (like a cigarette - BLAH!) Wrap the log in cellophane. Refrigerate.

SERVING SUGGESTIONS:

Watch out for this tasty treat! Guaranteed to overwhelm your garlic craving. Don't eat it on a first date. Serve any time of year with various salsa on the side or alone.

Andrea Riha
Vermont City Marathon
Burlington, Vermont

Chicken Curry Tartlets

INGREDIENTS:

Tartlets:
purchase from a gourmet shop
Sauce:
1 sm. chopped onion
1 tblsp. butter
1 tblsp. curry paste, season to taste (usually found in gourmet or
    Thai shops)
1 tsp. tomato paste
1/2 cup red wine or chicken broth
1 bay leaf
1 tblsp. lemon juice
3 tblsp. apricot or orange preserves
1 1/4 cup mayonnaise
1/2 cup whipping cream, whipped
Chicken:
12 1/2 oz. chicken product, drained and flaked

DIRECTIONS:

Cook onion in butter until soft. Add curry paste, tomato paste, liquid, bay leaf & lemon juice. Cook for 10-15 minutes until reduced. When thick, add preserves. Stir. Remove bay leaf and toss. Press a sieve if you want a clear sauce, or leave as is for more texture. In a separate bowl, beat whipping cream. Fold in mayo. Fold in sauce. Add chicken. Fill tartlets. Keep refrigerated. Garnish before serving with parsley, lemon peel, or fresh tomato slices.

Recipe makes 48+ curry tartlets

> *Monica Ritschke*
> Women's Runs for Health
> Appleton, Wisconsin

Trail Food Pizza Snacks

INGREDIENTS:

1 lb. hamburger
1 lb. pork sausage
1 lb. Velveeta cheese
3 tblsp. Worcestershire sauce
2 loaves cocktail rye bread
2 tsp. oregano
pinch of garlic powder, salt & pepper to taste

DIRECTIONS:

Fry sausage, and then hamburger. Drain very well. Add other ingredients and simmer in pan or skillet, just until the cheese melts. Spread on the cocktail rye slices on cookie sheet. These can be wrapped & frozen or heated in 350° oven for approximately 20 minutes.

Makes about 60 snacks.

SERVING SUGGESTIONS:

Great served at parties or get-together as appetizers. The hamburger and pork sausage can be substituted with leaner varieties to ensure a healthier, less fattening snack.

Jon DeLano
St. Louis Track Club
St. Louis, Missouri

Sawtooth Salsa

INGREDIENTS:

2 cups (about 2 cans) drained canned black beans
1/3 cup finely diced red bell pepper
1/4 cup finely chopped purple onion (white is also fine)
1/4 cup finely diced unpeeled cucumber
2 tblsp. finely diced celery
2 tblsp. finely minced jalapeno pepper
1 tblsp. chopped fresh basil (dried is fine)
2 tblsp. olive oil
2 tblsp. tomato juice
2 tblsp. red wine vinegar
1 tblsp. fresh lemon juice
1 1/2 tsp. chopped fresh thyme (dried is fine)
1/2 tsp. chili powder
1/4 tsp. salt
1 crushed clove garlic (dried is fine)

DIRECTIONS:

Combine all ingredients (the more finely minced & chopped the ingredients are, the better the salsa will be) and stir well. Cover and chill at least 30 minutes.

Makes 3 cups

Joe Pointer
Beaverton, Oregon

Heart Break Hummus

INGREDIENTS:

2 1/2 cups cooked chick peas (garbanzo beans)(canned or cooked)
4-5 cloves garlic(crushed or finely chopped)
1/4-1/2 cup lemon juice(freshly squeezed)
2 tblsp. olive oil
1/4-1/2 cup plain yogurt
1 tsp. ground cumin
sesame oil to taste - by drops
salt to taste

DIRECTIONS:

Reserve some liquid from the beans. In food processor finely chop garlic, add chick peas and process until smooth and mealy, scrape sides. Add lemon juice, olive oil, yogurt & cumin. Add and process to taste the salt and sesame oil. If too thick, thin with more yogurt or reserved liquid.

SERVING SUGGESTIONS:

Serve with vegetables, crackers, chips, cheese, toasted garlic bread, pita bread pieces. Can also use in sandwiches, pita pockets or tortillas.

Paul Mahre
Big Mountain Race Team
Whitefish, Montana

Kooks

I N G R E D I E N T S :

36 bread rounds
36 cucumber circles
1 onion (sm.)
1 mayonnaise (1/2 pint)
1 Parmesan cheese (sm.)

D I R E C T I O N S :

Chop onion in blender. Drain thoroughly. Mix with mayonnaise & cheese.
Layer bread with cucumbers circles. Spread with the cheese mixture &
broil.

S E R V I N G   S U G G E S T I O N S :

Serve while warm. 1 slice of bread makes four bread rounds. Enjoy!

Mary Schudy
Missoula Road & Track Club
Missoula, Montana

Spinach Roll-Ups

INGREDIENTS:

1 pkg. chopped frozen spinach (or fresh) / thawed & excess water
   squeezed out
1 cup (16 oz) sour cream
1 cup mayonnaise
1 bottle bacon bits
3 chopped green onion (optional)
1 pkg. Uncle Dan dry dressing mix
1 can chopped water chestnuts
1 pkg. tortilla shells (corn or flour)

DIRECTIONS:

Mix the first 7 ingredients together well. Spread a thin layer of the mixture
on the package of tortilla shells & roll up shells. Let rolled up shells sit
overnight. Cut into bite-size pieces & serve.

SERVING SUGGESTIONS:

Must be made the night before serving. *To make a lighter version lite mayonnaise & sour cream can be used. If using fat free products it is better to
use one fat free and one lite product.

Janice Abramson
Early Bloomer's Run
Spokane, Washington

Middle Eastern Tabouli

INGREDIENTS:

1 cup water
1/4 tsp. salt
1/2 cup bulgar wheat
1/3 cup minced parsley
2 chopped scallions
1 med. chopped cucumber
1 cup chopped tomatoes
1/4 cup finely chopped mint
1/4 cup oil
1/4 cup fresh lemon juice

DIRECTIONS:

Soften wheat by soaking 1 hour in water. Drain well & press out excess water. Mix ingredients together thoroughly. Serve on lettuce leaves in individual dishes & with pita bread.

Rose Marie George
Arthritis Foundation - Turkey Trot
Las Vegas, Nevada

Feta Stuffed Pasta Shells

INGREDIENTS:

48 large pasta shells
3/4 cup crumbled feta cheese
3/4 cup finely diced red pepper
12 finely chopped & pitted black olives
2 tblsp. fresh chopped parsley
1/2 tsp. dried oregano

DIRECTIONS:

In a pot of boiling water, cook pasta shells as directed on package (till al dente). Rinse with cold water. Drain well, arrange shells on a large microwave safe serving dish. Set aside. In bowl, combine feta, red pepper, olives, walnuts, parsley and oregano. Fill each pasta shell with about 1 teaspoon of feta cheese mixture. Use toothpick to skewer each shell. Microwave stuffed shells at medium (50%) for about 4-5 minutes or until heated through.

Makes 48 appetizers.

Mary Ross Cox
Run with the Spirit
Greensburg, Pennsylvania

Croatian Burek

INGREDIENTS:

6 oz. Phyllo dough
5 tblsp. melted butter
6 oz. Feta or goat cheese
1 egg yolk
1/4 tsp. white pepper
1/8 tsp. nutmeg
1/4 cup chopped dill &/or parsley

DIRECTIONS:

Preheat oven to 350°. Place phyllo dough on work surface with short ends on sides, and long ends on bottom & top. Brush butter onto leaves & cut them into 4 in. wide strips. Stack buttered strips so they don't dry. Mash feta cheese with egg yolk, pepper, nutmeg, & dill or parsley. Layer 3 strips phyllo, brush with butter. Place 1 tablespoon cheese mixture in corner of strip & fold into triangles by bringing phyllo corner to opposite edge. Continue folding in triangle until filling is completely enclosed. Brush with butter & place on cookie sheet. Repeat for remaining triangles. Bake at 350° for 15-20 minutes until golden. Serve at room temperature.

Makes 16-20 Bureks

SERVING SUGGESTIONS:

A wonderful appetizer with wine or beer. A little "old country" flavor from my Yugoslavian heritage.

> *Melitta Singlaub*
> Event Marketing Group
> Grand Junction, Colorado

Chili, Chowder, Soup & Stew

Chili, Chowder, Soup & Stew

Washington "Dawg" Breath Chili

Smoky Mountain Marathon Chili

Chili John's Chili

After Race White Bean Chili

Jamie's Vigorous Vegetable Soup

Bean Soup

Chickpea and Swiss Chard Soup

Cheddar Chowder

Taco Twist Soup

Tortellini Soup

Vegetable Gazpacho Delight

Dee's Tortilla Soup

Spinach and Sausage Soup

Turkey Chili Cincinati Style

Turkey Chili

Chicken Salsa Soup

Bushnell Chicken Stew

Chicken Tortilla Soup

Vegetarian Chili

Illinois Sausage Corn Chowder

Cheesy Tomato Spanish Rice Soup

Minestrone Soup

Peppery Pumpkin Soup

Syracuse Charger Leek and Chickpea Soup

Tomato Florentine Soup

Winter Tomato Florentine Soup

Washington "Dawg" Breath Chili

INGREDIENTS:

2 med. size chopped onions
2 chopped green peppers
2 stalks chopped celery
3 lbs. lean hamburger
1 lb. cubed sirloin
4 cloves of minced garlic
pepper, oregano, garlic salt to taste
1 can tomato paste
1 can chopped tomatoes
1 can tomato sauce
1/2 can of beer
3 oz. chili powder
8 oz. of your favorite hot salsa
3 finely chopped Jalapeños

DIRECTIONS:

Cook the onion, green pepper and celery in enough oil to cover the bottom of a soup kettle Add the meat and brown, cooking about 15 minutes. Remove any excess grease add all the remaining ingredients, sprinkling the pepper and oregano to cover the top of the stew. Simmer 2 1/2 hours, stirring every 15-20 minutes.

Serves 8-10

SERVING SUGGESTIONS:

This can be served with saltines and a bit of cheese grated on top! Perfect on a cold winter day!

Jennifer Wathen & Tom Lally
Dawg Dash - University of Washington Alumni Association
Seattle, Washington

Smoky Mountain Marathon Chili

INGREDIENTS:

3 lb. uncased chorizo sausage
2-12 oz. (drained) cans chili beans
3 tsp. chili powder
2 tsp. cayenne pepper
2 tsp. dried cilantro
1 tsp. sugar
1 lrg. (chopped) Vidalia onion
5 med. (chopped) jalapeno peppers
1/2 cup ketchup
1/2 cup grape jelly
1 bottle dark beer
3 oz. Tequila
4 oz. grated sharp cheddar cheese
Tabasco sauce (optional-to taste)

DIRECTIONS:

Brown sausage in large skillet. Combine browned sausage with remaining ingredients in a large stock pot over medium heat, stirring occasionally. Simmer for 30 minutes.

Makes 8 servings.

SERVING SUGGESTIONS:

Ladle into bowls and sprinkle with additional cheese. Garnish with a dollop of sour cream. Add Tabasco sauce to taste. Use nonflammable silverware. NOT recommended as a pre-race meal!

> *Sherman Ames*
> Knoxville Track Club
> Knoxville, Tennessee

Chili John's Chili

INGREDIENTS:

2 lb. hamburger meat
1 med. diced onion
1 tsp. white pepper
1 tsp. garlic powder
1 tblsp. cumin
1 tblsp. accent
1 tblsp. paprika
3 tblsp. chili powder
3 tsp. crushed red pepper
1 square unsweetened chocolate
2 cups cold water

DIRECTIONS:

Brown hamburger meat & onions. Add salt & pepper to taste. Mix in spices and add 2 cups water. Let simmer for a few hours. If desired, you can add mushrooms & hot peppers.

SERVING SUGGESTIONS:

This is the meat sauce for some incredible chili. Make spaghetti, grated cheese & beans, and spoon meat sauce over spaghetti. Sprinkle with oyster crackers. This hurts so good. Have plenty of cold beverages to control heat! Enjoy.

John Falk
Lakes Area Running Club
Burlington, Wisconsin

After Race White Bean Chili

INGREDIENTS:

1 lb. white beans(navy)
6 cups chicken broth
2 minced cloves garlic
2 med. chopped onions
1 tsp. oil
2-4 oz cans mild green chilies
2 tsp. ground cumin
1 1/2 tsp. oregano
1/4 tsp. ground cloves
1/4 tsp. cayenne pepper (red)
4 cups dried cooked chicken breast
3 cups grated Monterey Jack cheese
salsa
sour cream
chopped green onions with tops

DIRECTIONS:

Simmer chicken in water with a little celery & onion until done. Combine beans, broth, garlic and 1/2 onions in large soup pot. Bring to boil. Reduce heat, simmer until beans are soft (3 hours or more adding more broth if needed). In skillet sauté remaining onions in oil until tender. Add green chilies and seasoning and mix thoroughly. Add bean to mixture and add chicken and simmer 1 hour.

Serves 8-10 hungry runners

SERVING SUGGESTIONS:

Serve nice and HOT! Have cheese, salsa, sour cream & chopped green onions in separate bowls to offer as a topping for hot chili - ENJOY!

> *Ann M.Knight*
> Pensacola Runners Association
> Pensacola, Florida

Jamie's Vigorous Vegetable Soup

INGREDIENTS:

2 qts. water
4-5 carrots
5-6 russet potatoes
4 stalks celery
1 can corn
1/2 head cabbage
4-5 tomato bouillon
2 tomatoes (optional)
1/2 brown onion (optional)
2 cups Rice instead of potatoes (optional)

* Amount of vegetables may vary according to taste.

DIRECTIONS:

Dissolve tomato bouillon in boiling water. Peel potatoes and carrots. Chop vegetables to bite size. Add vegetables to boiling water. Cover and allow to cook over low heat for 45 minutes to an hour. Add salt and pepper to taste.

*Can be cooked in crock pot with allowing more cooking time.

Jamie Whitmore
Cal State Northridge Cross Country and Track
Elk Grove, California

Bean Soup

INGREDIENTS:

1 lb. ground meat
green onions
1 pkg. dry ranch dressing
1 pkg. taco seasoning
1 can whole kernel corn(drained)
1 can black beans with juice
1 can chili beans with juice
1 can pinto beans with juice
1 can Ro-tel tomatoes
1-16 oz. can chopped tomatoes

DIRECTIONS:

Brown ground meat & onions. Drain and add other ingredients. Cook 1 hour and serve with mexican corn bread.

SERVING SUGGESTIONS:

Serve with Mexican Corn bread: 2 pkgs. Jiffy mix corn bread - Follow directions on package and add: 1 can cream corn, chopped jalapeno peppers, grated sharp cheddar cheese, and a dollop of sour cream.

Buddy Graves
The Family YMCA
Hattiesburg, Mississippi

Chickpea and Swiss Chard Soup

INGREDIENTS:

1 bunch (1/2 lb.) Swiss chard
2 flat anchovy fillets
2 sm. sprigs fresh rosemary
1/3 cup extra virgin olive oil
4 peeled cloves of garlic
1 finely chopped onion
1 finely chopped carrot
1 can (15.5 oz.) plum tomatoes -
drain and crush by squeezing
through fingers
2 cans (15.5 oz.) drained chickpeas

1 cube chicken broth
water
salt
black pepper
1/2 cup sm. size pasta, such as
orzo, farfalline, or small wheels
Topping:
1/4 cup fresh grated Parmesan
cheese
olive oil

DIRECTIONS:

Cut off the tough ends of the chard stems and trim spoiled leaves. Wash thoroughly. Bring 2 cups of water to a boil, add teaspoon of salt and cook the chard until wilted and tender. Drain and reserve the cooking liquid. Chop chard coarsely. Mince anchovies and half of the rosemary leaves. In a heavy bottomed soup pot, heat olive oil and gently cook 2 of the garlic cloves until the garlic turns light brown or gold. Be careful not to burn garlic. Remove garlic and add minced anchovy. Add 1/2 the rosemary, chopped onion and carrot. Sauté until vegetables soften. Put the drained, crushed tomatoes and chopped chard in the pot and cook a few minutes, mixing them well with the other vegetables and oil. Add the chickpeas, broth cube, and the reserved chard cooking liquid to the pot. Add more water to cover all the ingredients well, about a quart or so (add more to maintain a "soupy" consistency as it cooks). Season with a teaspoon of salt and a generous amount of fresh ground black pepper. Simmer for at least a half an hour. While the soup cooks, finely mince remaining 2

cloves of garlic and other half of the rosemary. Pureé about half of the soup in a food mill or processor and return to the pot. Bring to a boil and add pasta. When the pasta is cooked (al dente), turn off the heat and add minced garlic and rosemary. Taste and correct salt and pepper, if necessary.

Note: You can substitute ingredients, i.e. kale for chard, cannellini beans for chickpeas. But this is my preferred combination, and I have successfully made this by using Progresso beans and tomatoes.

SERVING SUGGESTIONS:

Serve in bowls with a sprinkle of Parmesan cheese and a drizzle of extra virgin oil on top. Good bread should accompany this feast.

Marilyn L. Nicholson
Volcano Art Center's Kilauea Volcano
Wilderness & Rim Runs
Hawaii National Park, Hawaii

Cheddar Chowder

INGREDIENTS:

2 cups boiling water
2 cups cauliflower-florets
1 cup diced potatoes
1/2 cup sliced carrots
1/2 cup sliced celery
1/4 cup chopped onion
1 1/2 tsp. salt
1/4 tsp. pepper
1/4 cup butter or margarine
1/4 cup flour
2 cups milk
2 cups shredded mild or sharp cheddar cheese

DIRECTIONS:

In saucepan combine water, vegetables, salt & pepper. Cover & simmer 10 minutes. Do not drain. In large sauce pan, melt butter stir in flour, then milk & heat to boiling. Continue simmering, stirring constantly until thickened. Add cheddar cheese & stir until melted. Add undrained vegetables. Heat through but do not boil.

Serves 8

SERVING SUGGESTIONS:

Yum, yum, yum. Excellent soup for all to enjoy.

> *Thomas J. Deloyr*
> The Brian Douglas Memorial Lincolnshire
> Community Association 5K Race
> Lincolnshire, Illinois

Taco Twist Soup

INGREDIENTS:

1 lb. lean ground beef
1 med. chopped onion
2 cloves minced garlic
1-2 tsp. chili powder, as desired
1 tsp. ground cumin
3 cups beef broth
1 1/2 cups picante sauce
1 (14 1/2 oz.) can diced tomatoes in juice
1 cup uncooked rotini pasta
1 sm. chopped green pepper
shredded cheddar cheese
tortilla chips

DIRECTIONS:

In large saucepan or Dutch oven, brown ground beef with onion & garlic, (drain). Sprinkle chili powder & cumin over meat; cook & stir 30 seconds. Add remaining ingredients except cheese & tortilla chips; mix well. Bring to a boil, stirring frequently. Reduce heat, cover & simmer 10 to 15 minutes or until pasta is tender, stirring occasionally. Ladle into bowls; top with cheese. Serve with tortilla chips & additional picante sauce.

Makes about 8 (1 cup) servings.

Carol Gilbert
Quakerdale Cedar Valley Race
Iowa Falls, Iowa

Tortellini Soup

INGREDIENTS:

2 cloves garlic minced
1 tblsp. margarine
3 cans low fat chicken broth
1-10 oz. pkg. spinach thawed & drained
1-16 oz. can stewed tomatoes undrained & coarsely chopped
1-8 oz. bag of cheese tortellini

DIRECTIONS:

Sauté garlic in margarine 2-3 minutes. Add broth & tortellini, and heat to a boil. Reduce heat, simmer for 10 minutes. Add spinach & tomatoes, simmer 5 minutes.

SERVING SUGGESTIONS:

Top with grated cheese & serve with crusty italian bread. Its great after a cold run.

Robert and Linda Hyer
Freehold Running Club
Marlboro, New Jersey

Vegetable Gazpacho Delight

INGREDIENTS:

1-16 oz. can corn
4 tomatoes
1 onion
2 cucumber
4 carrots
2 green peppers
1 tblsp. chopped parsley
1/4 cup vinegar
1/4 cup olive oil
1-46 oz can V-8 tomato juice

DIRECTIONS:

Peel tomatoes after boiling for 30 seconds. Chop coarsely & separately in food processor; corn, peeled tomatoes, onion, cucumber, carrots, green pepper & fresh parsley. Put all chopped vegetables & vinegar together in food processor & chop for 15 seconds so that vegetables are mixed & still coarsely chopped. Add tomato juice or V-8 mixed with chopped vegetables upon serving.

SERVING SUGGESTIONS:

Chill or refrigerate mixture & tomato juice before serving. Mix tomato juice with mixture to consistency of your choice upon serving.

*Note: I ran my personal best when I ate this gazpacho once or twice a week.

Irvin M. Miller
Mid Hudson Road Runners Club
Poughkeepsie, New York

Dee's Tortilla Soup

INGREDIENTS:

10 corn tortillas
1 tblsp. vegetable oil
1 med. chopped onion
1 tsp. minced fresh garlic
8 cups chicken broth
2 cups diced chicken (or white fish)
1/2 tsp. ground cumin
1 med. green, yellow and red bell peppers - seeded and cut into strips.
2 tblsp. chopped fresh cilantro
2 med. chopped tomatoes
1 med. avocado peeled and diced
1-6 oz. pkg. grated Monterey Jack cheese
1 cup med. or hot salsa
Garnish: sour cream (optional), cilantro (optional)

DIRECTIONS:

Heat oven to 400 degrees. Spray both sides of tortillas with non stick cooking spray. Stack & cut into 1/2 inch wide strips, then cut in half crosswise. Spread strips evenly on ungreased baking sheet and bake 8-10 minutes turning once, until crisp and brown. Remove pan from oven. Let cool. Heat oil in a 4-6 quart pot. Add onion & garlic and cook over medium - low heat 3-4 minutes stirring until softened. Add broth, chicken or fish, & cumin. Bring to boil over high heat. Add bell peppers. Reduce heat & boil gently 5 minutes, or until peppers are crisp tender. Stir in cilantro. Divide tortilla strips, tomatoes, avocados, cheese & salsa among bottoms of 4-6 bowls. Ladle soup into bowls & top with sour cream. Sprinkle with cilantro. Serve with warm tortillas.

Serves 4-6

Deanne Denholme
Once Around Lake Cavanugh
Seattle, Washington

Spinach and Sausage Soup

INGREDIENTS:

8 tblsp. butter or margarine
1 cup chopped onion
1/2 cup flour
2 cans beef bouillon (10 1/2 oz. slice)
1 1/2 cups water
2 cups Half & Half or evaporated milk
1-8 oz. pkg. brown & serve sliced frozen sausages
2-10 oz. pkgs. thawed & drained frozen chopped spinach
1 tsp. salt
1/2 tsp. sugar
1/4 tsp. black pepper
1/4 tsp. nutmeg

DIRECTIONS:

Heat butter in large skillet until melted. Add onion & cook until tender. Add flour & stir until smooth. Add beef bouillon & water. Heat, stirring until mixture comes to a boil. Add Half & Half, sausage & spinach; return to a boil. Reduce heat & simmer 10 minutes. Add salt, pepper, sugar & nutmeg. Serve with pumpernickel.

Makes 2 quarts.

SERVING SUGGESTIONS:

This is a lunchtime favorite when our family is skiing at Breckinridge Colorado.

Susan Alexander
Mesa Monument Striders
Whitewater, Colorado

Turkey Chili Cincinnati Style

INGREDIENTS:

1 lb. ground turkey
1 pkg. Williams chili mix - use the one designed for 2 lbs. of meat
1 lrg. can whole tomatoes
1 can diced tomatoes
1 can chili beans including the sauce
1 can drained dark kidney beans
2 tsp. ground cinnamon (WHOA! I'm not kidding)
salt & pepper to taste

DIRECTIONS:

In a large dutch oven or soup pot, bring 2 quarts of salted water to a boil.
Add 1 lb. of ground turkey. Break up turkey as it boils to a crumble consistency. Boil for approximately 5 minutes or until the turkey is light brown.
Drain. (Note: Don't be alarmed if there is a white foam substance on your
turkey, just drain and rinse off. I also like to rinse out the dutch oven
because the foam gives me the creeps!) Return the drained turkey to the
dutch oven and add all other ingredients. Bring everything to a boil for 10
minutes, then reduce to a medium low heat. Let simmer for 30 minutes to 2
hours. Depending on when your next meal is!

SERVING SUGGESTIONS:

Serve over cooked spaghetti, topped with diced onion and shredded cheese.

Jane Deterding
Race for Justice
Wichita, Kansas

Turkey Chili

INGREDIENTS:

1 med. chopped onion
2-2 1/2 lbs. turkey
2-14.5 oz. canned tomatoes
2 tsp. chili powder
1/4 cup soy sauce
generous dash of garlic powder
1-15 oz. can of kidney, pinto, chili beans
2 tblsp. vegetable or canola oil

DIRECTIONS:

In a large Dutch oven, sauté onion in oil until tender, crumble ground turkey & add to onion & oil. Brown. Drain fat. Add canned tomatoes with juices, breaking up the whole tomatoes. Add chili powder, garlic salt, soy sauce. Cover and reduce heat to low. Cook for 30 minutes. Add beans, with liquids. Simmer for another 10-15 minutes until heated thoroughly.

SERVING SUGGESTIONS:

Serve in bowl, with grated cheese and crackers, or pour over pasta or cooked rice. For a spicer chili, add red pepper to taste, a dash of salt & cumin.

Mark Lidman
Blue Springs Runners - KC Northland Runners
Blue Springs, Missouri

Chicken Salsa Soup

INGREDIENTS:

4 chicken breast
1 pint salsa (medium or mild)
2 cans corn
1/2 cup diced green pepper
4 tsp. chili powder
broth from chicken
tortilla chips
Monterey Jack cheese (shredded)

DIRECTIONS:

Cook chicken in Dutch oven in 4-8 cups of water depending on how much soup you want to make. Remove chicken and tear in to small bite size pieces. Add salsa, corn, green peppers & chili powder to broth. Return chicken to the mixture. Simmer until ready to serve.

SERVING SUGGESTIONS:

I like it better when less water is used. Top each bowl with a sprinkle of Monterey Jack Cheese. Serve with tortilla chips on the side.

Greg Hipp
Charlotte Road Runners Club
Charlotte, North Carolina

Bushnell Chicken Stew

INGREDIENTS:

olive oil
1 coarsely chopped onion
2 coarsely chopped bell peppers
1 sm. coarsely chopped fennel bulb
1 cup quartered mushrooms
3 lrg. cloves crushed garlic
2 1/2 cups white wine
4 cups coarsely chopped ripe
  tomatoes
1 tsp. salt
2 tblsp. dried basil

1/4 tsp. dried red pepper flakes
1/2 tsp. dried rosemary
1/2 tsp. dried thyme
1/4 tsp. dried sage
1/4 tsp. Chinese 5 Spice
freshly ground pepper to taste
6 thickly sliced carrots
4 whole boneless, skinless chicken
  breasts

DIRECTIONS:

Pour enough oil into a large stew pot to cover bottom. Heat over medium heat. Add onion, bell peppers, fennel, mushrooms & garlic. Cook, stirring often until onion is translucent. Add wine, tomatoes and seasonings. Turn heat to high and bring to a boil, then reduce heat to low and simmer at least 10 minutes (up to several hours). Adjust seasonings to taste. Add carrots. Cook on low heat 20 minutes. Cut chicken into chunks. Add to stew pot and cook thoroughly.

SERVING SUGGESTIONS:

Serve in large bowls, garnish with fronds from fennel. Serve with warm, fresh bread.

Jeanette & Richard Albright
Club Northwest
Edmonds, Washington

Chicken Tortilla Soup

INGREDIENTS:

2 lbs. boneless chicken breast
2 tblsp. oil
1 cup chopped celery
2 med. chopped onions
5 cloves minced garlic
5 cans Swanson vegetable broth
2 cans (14 1/2 oz. size) Swanson low fat chicken broth
2 cans Del Monte stewed tomatoes (Mexican style)
1 can Ro-tel tomatoes & chilies
2 tblsp. ground cumin
Ortega chopped jalapenos (optional)
white corn tortilla chips
string cheese cut into 1/2" chunks

DIRECTIONS:

Cut chicken breasts into "nugget" size chunks and brown in oil in non-stick skillet. While chicken browns, bring broth to a boil. Add onions, garlic, celery, browned chicken and cumin. Cook 30 minutes. Add stewed & Ro-tel tomatoes. Cook another 20 minutes. If not "hot" enough, add jalapeños to taste.

SERVING SUGGESTIONS:

Place a handful of chips in each bowl. Ladle soup and top with chunks of cheese.

Shirley & John Haugh
Tri-Rivers Running Club
Salina, Kansas

Vegetarian Chili

INGREDIENTS:

1 cup dried lentils
1-15 oz. can pinto beans
1-15 oz. can spicy chili beans
3 cups water
1 tsp. olive oil
2 cloves minced garlic
2 cups chopped onion
2 tblsp. chili powder
2 cans (14 1/2 oz. each) stewed tomatoes
1-8 oz. can tomato sauce
1 tsp. salt (optional)
green chilies (optional)

DIRECTIONS:

Wash & pick over lentils to discard any debris. In a large saucepan, cover lentils with water & bring to a boil. Reduce heat, cover and simmer for 30 minutes or until tender & water is absorbed. Coat large non-stick skillet with cooking spray. Heat oil to medium-hot and brown garlic & onions for 5 minutes. Add to lentils, along with all other ingredients. Simmer for an additional 45 minutes or until flavors are well blended. Thin out with water if too thick. Serve hot.

Makes about 4-5 cups.

SERVING SUGGESTIONS:

Serve with hot, crusty bread and a cold glass of skim milk on the side for a power-packed, delicious meal.
*For spicier chili, substitute 1 can of tomatoes with green chilies for 1 of the 2 cans of stewed tomatoes

Golda E. Ewalt, RD
Central Illinois Dietetic Association
Peoria, Illinois

Illinois Sausage Corn Chowder

INGREDIENTS:

1 lb. bulk pork sausage
1 cup chopped onions
4 cups-1/2 inch cubes of peeled potatoes
1 tsp. salt
2 cups water
1-17 oz. can cream style corn
1-17 oz. can drained whole kernel corn
1-12 oz. can evaporated milk

DIRECTIONS:

Brown sausage and onion. Drain and add potatoes, salt & water. Bring to boil; reduce heat and simmer about 15 minutes. Add corn & evaporated milk. Heat.

SERVING SUGGESTIONS:

Serve with warm French bread, spread with butter. Enjoy!

Marcia Lintz
Firecracker Run
East Moline, Illinois

Cheesy Tomato Spanish Rice Soup

INGREDIENTS:

2 cups water
3/4 cup uncooked brown rice
2 cups finely chopped celery
1 1/2 cups dried carrots
2 tblsp. divided chili powder
8 cups tomato puree*
4 oz. (1/2 cup) canned mild green chilies
2 1/2 tsp. ground cumin
1/2 tsp. granulated garlic

1 lrg. chopped tomato
1/4 lb. small cubes cheddar cheese
1/2 cup sour cream (low or non-fat)
3/4 cup diced green onions

*Tomato Puree: Blend 4 lbs. chopped unpeeled tomatoes until smooth (canned tomatoes may be used)

DIRECTIONS:

Cook rice, celery, carrots and 1 tblsp. chili powder in water on low heat, covered for 1/2 hour. Add blended tomato puree & chilies. Bring to a second boil. Simmer covered for 15 minutes, stirring occasionally. Add water if too thick. Add remaining chili powder, cumin, garlic & fresh tomatoes. Simmer for 10 minutes. Turn burner to lowest heat. Add cheese, sour cream; stir quickly. Heat gently for 5 minutes.

Serves 8

SERVING SUGGESTIONS:

Serve hot in bowl. Top with a dollop of sour cream. Sprinkle with sliced green onions. *Optional: Use hot pepper cheese instead of cheddar for an extra zing! This fun soup is great to serve at the beginning of any Mexican or international meal, or as a meal itself with warmed flour or corn tortillas and a mixed green salad!

Cathy Myers
Dayspring Christian Academy
New Providence, Pennsylvania

Minestrone Soup

INGREDIENTS:

1 lb. lean beef stew meat
6 cups water
1 can (28 oz.) cup up tomatoes with liquid
1 beef bouillon cube
1 med. chopped onion
2 tblsp. minced dried parsley
2 1/2 tsp. salt (optional)
1 1/2 tsp. ground thyme
1/2 tsp. pepper
1 med. thinly sliced zucchini
2 cup finely chopped cabbage
1 can (16 oz.) drained garbanzo beans
1 cup uncooked elbow or shell macaroni (sm.)
1/4 cup grated parmesan cheese (optional)

DIRECTIONS:

In a slow cooker combine beef, water, tomatoes, bouillon, onion, parsley, salt if desired, thyme & pepper. Cover & cook on low for 7-9 hours or until meat is tender. Add zucchini, cabbage, beans & macaroni. Cover & cook on high for 30-45 minutes more or until the vegetables are tender. Sprinkle individual servings with parmesan cheese if desired.

Makes 8 servings

Carol Gilbert
Quakerdale Cedar Valley Race
Iowa Falls, Iowa

Peppery Pumpkin Soup

INGREDIENTS:

2 cups boiled & drained pumpkin (or acorn squash)
2 tsp. margarine
1/2 med. diced onion
1/2 tsp. salt
1 tsp. cayenne pepper
1/2 tsp. black pepper
2 cubes chicken bouillon w/2 cups water (*or 2-6oz. cans chicken broth)
4 tsp. sour cream

DIRECTIONS:

Melt margarine & brown onions until clear. Add spices, chicken bouillon & water. Heat & stir until dissolved. Add pumpkin. Heat through & blend until smooth. Add water to soup to desired thickness.

SERVING SUGGESTIONS:

Top with sour cream. Enjoy!

Amol Saxena
Juana Run 5 mile
Palo Alto, California

Syracuse Charger Leek and Chickpea Soup

INGREDIENTS:

2 1/2 lbs. leeks
3 tblsp. extra virgin olive oil
salt
1-16 oz. can chickpeas(drained)
2 beef bouillon cubes
freshly ground black pepper
1/2 cup grated cheese(optional)
*Crusty bread

DIRECTIONS:

Trim away root ends of leeks. Cut into thin disks and soak in cold water. Shake dry. Put leeks into medium saucepan, add olive oil & salt. Heat at medium-low and cover, turning over until leeks and nearly dissolved. While leeks cook, squeeze off chickpea peels with your fingers. Add chickpeas, bouillon and enough water to cover all by 2" to leeks in pot. Mix all with wooden spoon and cover. Cook for another 15 minutes. Take 2-3 ladle fulls out of soup and puree in blender or processor. Add pepper to swirling mixture (and add cheese if desired). Return it to saucepan for 5 more minutes of cooking. Serve!

Makes 4 ample or 6 moderate servings.

SERVING SUGGESTIONS:

You may prepare everything even a day in advance up to, but not including, the moment when you add the pepper & or cheese. You can also add chopped spinach to the leeks for a more pronounced healthy green color.

Mickey Dockwiller
Syracuse Chargers Track Club
Liverpool, New York

Tomato Florentine Soup

INGREDIENTS:

1-28 oz. can diced tomatoes (Hunts)
1 qt. defatted chicken or turkey broth
3 cloves garlic
1 chopped onion
2 chopped potatoes
5-6 chopped celery stalks
1 cup (or more) chopped spinach
6-8 oz rotini or other pasta (I like whole wheat when I can get it)
2 tblsp. olive oil
salt & pepper to taste

DIRECTIONS:

Sauté onions & garlic in olive oil in a large pot. Add broth & tomatoes. Simmer for about 30 minutes. Add potatoes & celery. Simmer another 30 minutes. Add spinach & pasta shells & boil until pasta is soft. Serve immediately with corn bread (homemade of course)! This is delicious!

Pat Nelson
Nashville Striders
Murfreesboro, Tennessee

Winter Tomato Florentine Soup

INGREDIENTS:

1 lrg. can of chicken broth (College Inn brand recommended)
2 sm. cans of Del Monte stewed tomatoes
1 frozen block of chopped spinach
1 pkg. frozen cheese tortellini or pastina (any kind)
1 canister of Romano cheese
1 loaf of Italian bread
Seasoning:
> Basil
> Garlic
> Oregano

DIRECTIONS:

Pour large can of chicken broth in cooking pot. Add stewed tomatoes - I like to whirl the stewed tomatoes first in a blender - This breaks up the tomato chunks and provides a smoother consistency. Bring contents to a boil and add frozen spinach
*I use the whole block of spinach since I like spinach; however, you may want to use only half the block. Season to preference with basil, garlic and oregano Stir in the pastina or tortellini. Cover and simmer until the pastina or tortellini is cooked. Your soup is now ready!

SERVING SUGGESTIONS:

Place in a bowl with a little romano cheese on top
If you like, serve with crusty Italian bread and a salad of your choice
Bon- appetite!

> *John C. Brown*
> Lebo 5K
> Mt. Lebanon, Pennsylvania

Beef & Pork

Beef and Pork

Mountain Man Meatloaf

Pittsburgh Power Meal

Flank Steak on the Grill

Skillet Enchiladas

Barbeque Brisket

Southern Indiana Pork Chops

Taco Lasagna

Franklin's Finish Pastry

Pork Posole

Red Beans and Rice

Jill's Jambalaya

Crazy Portland Marathon Meatballs

Mountain Man Meatloaf

INGREDIENTS:

2 lbs. very lean ground beef
2 eggs
1/2 cup finely chopped onion
1 finely chopped green pepper
1 1/2 cups uncooked oatmeal
1 tblsp. Worcestershire sauce
1 1/2 tsp. dry mustard
1 tsp. salt
1/2 tsp. pepper
3/4 cup (1 sm. can) vegetable juice cocktail
8 oz. can tomato sauce
4 oz. can diced drained jalapeños

DIRECTIONS:

Preheat oven to 350°. Mix together all but the last 2 ingredients. In a shallow casserole or baking dish, mold ingredients into a bomb-shaped loaf about 9" long and 4" high. Pour tomato sauce over top. Bake uncovered 1 hour, 15 minutes. Remove from oven, and sprinkle diced jalapeños over the top.

SERVING SUGGESTIONS:

I live in 9000 ft high Cloudcroft, NM, site of the world's highest certified 10K race - the *Governor Gary Johnson 10K Run and Walk*. We enjoy cold winters and cool summers, so a spicy meatloaf tastes good any time of the year. I serve mine with baked potatoes, fresh corn-on-the-cob and green salad, with chocolate frozen yogurt for dessert.

Don L. Hoffman
Governor Gary Johnson 10K Run/Walk
Cloudcroft, New Mexico

Pittsburgh Power Meal

INGREDIENTS:

1-8" piece of polish smoked sausage
1-6" sandwich bun
1 can of sauerkraut
1 ear of corn
1 baked potato
1 can chili baked beans
lots of butter
several cans of Iron City Beer
mustard (optional)

DIRECTIONS:

Run 10 miles. Turn on Pittsburgh Pirates game. Drink a few Iron City Beers. Have a friend or relative cook all the food to your specifications. Go for it!

SERVING SUGGESTIONS:

The further you can run the better the Iron City Beer will taste. Never prepare the food yourself because it always tastes better when someone else makes it. Put the beans in some kind of container so they don't get everywhere. Too much sauerkraut will make the buns too soft. Distance runners need plenty of fat in their diets. When in doubt, drink another beer.

John Papa
Slippery Rock University
Grove City, Pennsylvania

Flank Steak on the Grill

INGREDIENTS:

2-1 1/2 lb. flank steaks
2-3 cloves garlic
1-1" piece of ginger
1 onion
1 tblsp. ground cumin
1 tsp. dried oregano
2 tblsp. soy sauce
2 tsp. dry sherry
1 tsp. pepper
juice of 1 lemon
1/4 cup red wine
1/4 cup olive oil

DIRECTIONS:

Pulse marinade ingredients in blender. Marinate steaks in a plastic bag overnight. Prepare grill. When coals are red hot place steaks on grill 5-6 minutes on one side, 3-4 minutes on the other side. Slice across the grain on the bias into thin slices.

Serves 5-6 hungry people

SERVING SUGGESTIONS:

Can be served with salsa & grilled red peppers & onions, wrapped in flour burritos as fajitas.

Pastor Rick Lawrence
Moving in the Right Direction
Rome, Wisconsin

Skillet Enchiladas

INGREDIENTS:

1 lb. ground beef
1/2 cup red onions
1-10 3/4 oz. can cream of mushroom soup
1-10 oz. can enchilada sauce
1/3 cup milk
2 tblsp. diced green chili peppers
12 corn tortillas
3 cups shredded cheese - (can be cheddar or 1/2 cheddar, 1/2 jack)

DIRECTIONS:

In electric skillet brown ground beef and onions. Drain. Stir in mushroom soup, enchilada sauce, milk & chilies. Bring to bubbling mixture @ 325°. Reduce heat to 225°. Cover and cook for 20 minutes. Stir occasionally. Soften tortillas in microwave. Fill center with cheese and roll. Place in skillet. Cover and cook for 5 minutes. Turn each tortilla so sauce covers each side. Sprinkle cheese on top.

Angela Jimerson
Autumn Color Run
Buena Vista, Colorado

Barbeque Brisket

INGREDIENTS:

1 4-5 lb. Brisket
garlic powder
minced onion
celery seed
2-3 oz. liquid smoke
pepper
Worcestshire sauce
Sauce:
1 cup ketchup
1 cup water
2 dashes Tabasco sauce
1 tsp. chili powder
3 tblsp. Worcestshire sauce

DIRECTIONS:

Sprinkle brisket with garlic, onion and celery seed. Place in a glass or crockery baking dish. Pour on the liquid smoke. Cover and let marinate overnight in the refrigerator. In the morning sprinkle with black pepper and Worcestshire sauce. Bake @ 250° for 5 hours with lid on. Lift out of juices. Cool on platter, slice-but not entirely through. Pour out juices and place back in pan. Pour on barbeque sauce and bake 30-45 minutes. Remove lid last 10 minutes. Mix sauce ingredients, then simmer covered for 20 minutes.

Angela Schultz
Colorado Springs Race For The Cure
Colorado Springs, Colorado

Southern Indiana Pork Chops

INGREDIENTS:

2 cups soy sauce
1/2 cup brown sugar
1 tblsp. Black Strap molasses or Bead molasses
1 cup water
1" thick pork chops

DIRECTIONS:

Mix marinade ingredients and marinate chops in refrigerator for 8 to 24 hours before grilling.

SERVING SUGGESTIONS:

This special sauce makes a juicy & tasty chop.

Nancy Johnson
University of Southern Indiana Eagle 5K Run/Walk
Evansville, Indiana

Taco Lasagna

INGREDIENTS:

1 lb. lean ground beef
1 pkg. taco seasoning
1 can refried beans
1 pkg. corn of flour tortillas (soft)
12 oz. shredded taco cheese
2 lrg. jars salsa
1 chopped onion
1 head shredded lettuce

DIRECTIONS:

Brown ground beef & 1/2 onion in a skillet and drain well. In large saucepan heat the refried beans, and the other 1/2 onion. Cut tortillas into 1" strips. Put a little salsa in the bottom of the baking dish. Layer 1/3 tortillas, 1/3 beans, 1/3 meat, 1/3 cheese, 1/3 salsa. Repeat until all of the ingredients are used. Bake @ 350° for 20 minutes. Serve on shredded lettuce.

Dean Kessler
Careyfest Twilight 5-K
Carey, Ohio

Franklin's Finnish Pastry

INGREDIENTS:

6 lrg. thinly sliced potatoes(peeled)
1 chopped onion
1 lb. coarse ground lean beef
1/4 tsp. black pepper
1 tsp. salt (optional)
2 sliced carrots (optional)

Crust:
2 1/2 cups flour
3/4 cup margarine
6 tblsp. cold water (as needed to hold crusts together)

DIRECTIONS:

Mix filling ingredients together and divide into 4 equal portions. Make crust by combining all ingredients. Divide into 4 equal portions. Roll each of them out as if making a pie crust. Put 1/4 filling into each individual pie crust. Fold the crust over the ingredients an all sides. Seal edges and by using a fork poke several holes into the top of the crusts so the steam can escape. Bake @ 350° for approximately 1 hour, or until crust is golden brown and meat & potatoes are completely cooked.

SERVING SUGGESTIONS:

Delicious when eaten with ketchup and a side salad.

Don Franklin
South Wood County YMCA Striders
Wisconsin Rapids, Wisconsin

Pork Posole

INGREDIENTS:

8 pork steaks
2 cups canned tomatoes
1 onion
1/2 tsp. garlic salt
8 oz. chopped green chili
2 lrg. cans hominy
2 tblsp. olive oil

DIRECTIONS:

Cut meat into bite-size chunks. Flour and brown in skillet with oil. Chop tomatoes, dice onion. Combine all ingredients in large pan & simmer at least 5 hours. Freezes well.

SERVING SUGGESTIONS:

Serve with tortillas and beer.

John E. Farrow
Albuquerque Road Runners Club
Albuquerque, New Mexico

Red Beans and Rice

INGREDIENTS:

1 lb. dried red beans
2 lbs. smoked linked sausage or reduced fat turkey sausage
1 lrg. chopped onion
1 lrg. chopped bell pepper
2 tsp. salt
1 tsp. garlic powder
1 tsp. lemon pepper seasoning
2 bay leaves
4 drops Zatarian's shrimp boil
1 can Ro-tel tomatoes

DIRECTIONS:

Rinse & sort beans. Let soak a few hours or overnight. Chop sausage in bite-size pieces. Combine all ingredients in Dutch oven or large soup pot. Cover with water by about 2"; bring to a boil. Reduce to low heat and let simmer for 2 1/2 to 3 hours, until beans are tender & juice thickens. For thicker gravy, remove lid and turn to high; or mash some of the beans & return to pot.

SERVING SUGGESTIONS:

Serve over cooked rice. Great with corn bread.

Johnny Dye
Tupelo Running Club
Tupelo, Mississippi

Jill's Jambalaya

INGREDIENTS:

2 lrg. chopped red onions
1 chopped green bell pepper
5 chopped scallions
4 cloves chopped garlic
1 tblsp. cajun seasoning
1/2 tsp. cayenne pepper
1/2 tsp. oregano
2 bay leaves
1/2 cup cubed ham
1/2 cup cubed hot sausage - cooked
3 cups uncooked long grain rice
2 tblsp. tomato paste
1/2 cup butter
1 chopped jalapeño chili w/seeds
2-16 oz. cans chicken broth
1-28 oz. can stewed tomatoes

DIRECTIONS:

In a Dutch oven add butter, chopped red onion, bell pepper, 4 scallions, garlic, jalapeño, oregano, cayenne pepper, cajun seasoning & bay leaves. Stir and cook for 15 minutes or until the vegetables are cooked. Add tomato paste, chicken broth, stewed tomatoes, cooked meats, & rice. Simmer with cover until rice is cooked, stirring rice occasionally. Cooking time is 1 hour and until all the juice is cooked out. Place last chopped scallion on top as a garnish.

Jill Bender
WAGS (Wisconsin Academy for Graduate Service)
Janesville, Wisconsin

Crazy Portland Marathon Meatballs

INGREDIENTS:

2 lbs. lean ground beef
1 envelope dry onion soup mix
1/2 cup dry bread crumbs
3 eggs
1/2 cup water
1 cup brown sugar
1 can whole cranberry relish
1-12 oz. bottle chile sauce
1 cup strained sauerkraut

DIRECTIONS:

Mix ground beef, onion soup mix, bread crumbs and eggs. Form into meatballs and place raw in a 9"x13" pan. In a separate bowl, mix chili sauce, water, sauerkraut, sugar and cranberries. Then pour mixture over meatballs. Bake uncovered @ 350° for 1 1/2 hours.

SERVING SUGGESTIONS:

This is a weird combination but it creates great sweet & sour meatballs.

Les Smith
Portland Marathon Event Director
Portland, Oregon

From
the Sea

From The Sea

Back of the Pack Shrimp

10 Minute Seafood Pasta

Indiana Wesleyan Seafood Chowder

Heaven on a Plate

Down the Bayou

Citrus Salmon Bake

Portland Marathon Clam Chowder

Cajun Pasta

Greek Shrimp Over Rice

Seafood Chowder

Baked Alaska King Salmon

Skillet Shrimp & Sausage

MJ's Clam Chowder

Crawfish Etoufeé

Nantucket Bay Scallops in Pasta Shell

Wrightwood Smoked Salmon

Fish Creole

Seafood Pasta

Back of the Pack Shrimp

INGREDIENTS:

1 lb. fresh, whole shrimp
3 tblsp. olive oil
8 garlic cloves, peeled and cut into criss cross strips
3/4 tsp. red pepper flakes
1 cup dry white wine
1/4 cup minced parsley
1 cup chopped scallions

DIRECTIONS:

Pick the whole fresh shrimp up from your local seafood market. This includes heads, tails, fronts, backs, feelers, etc.; everything that makes a shrimp a shrimp. Beware of decapitated shrimp that have spent their last few months sitting in a warehouse in Chicago. They may play well in Peoria, but they don't cut the mustard in San Francisco. Heat the oil in a skillet and toss in the scallions. Let them cook for 2 minutes, then add garlic and shrimp. Cook until the shrimp are pink; pour in the wine and simmer for another minute. Remove the skillet from the heat and sprinkle in the parsley & pepper flakes. For convenience, serve directly from the skillet. Twist off heads & shells, don't be afraid to get your little pinkies in it, there's no other way out. Since this can be a bit messy, save the tuxedos & haute couture for another occasion. Scoop up some of the seasoning with a fork and then skewer the meat.

SERVING SUGGESTIONS:

Serve with steamed rice, salad, & sourdough bread to dip in the sauce.

Thomas Boyd
San Francisco Dolphin South End Running Club
San Francisco, California

10 Minute Seafood Pasta

INGREDIENTS:

2-3 tsp. olive oil
1/2 lb. fresh scallops
1/2 lb. med. cooked shrimp
1 tblsp. garlic (in jar)
1 tblsp. basil (in jar)
1 cup freshly sliced mushrooms
2-3 cans stewed tomatoes
Linguini pasta

DIRECTIONS:

Sauté scallops & shrimp in olive oil in large skillet or wok. Add garlic, basil, stirring until well mixed. Add stewed tomatoes and simmer 5-10 minutes while pasta cooks. Serve sauce over cooked pasta and garnish with grated cheese.

SERVING SUGGESTIONS:

This is a low fat, fast, and very tasty. A creation of my son, Kevin, an excellent athlete and great person.

Suzy Truax
Finish Line Productions, Inc.
Reno, Nevada

Indiana Wesleyan Seafood Chowder

INGREDIENTS:

1 lb. fresh shelled & deveined shrimp
3 slices diced bacon
1 med. chopped onion
1 chopped green pepper
1-10 oz. can clams with juice
5 cubed new potatoes
1 tblsp. instant chicken bouillon
1/2 tblsp. dried thyme
2 cup milk
1/4 cup flour
dash fresh ground pepper

DIRECTIONS:

In a Dutch oven, cook the bacon until crisp. Combine can of clams (with juice), potatoes, bouillon, pepper sauce, thyme & pepper; set aside. Cook onion & green pepper with bacon. Add clam & potato mixture to Dutch oven. Bring to boil, then reduce heat. Simmer gently, uncovered, until potatoes are tender (about 15 minutes). Combine milk & flour. Whisk into pan. Bring to boiling, stirring frequently, then reduce heat. Add shrimp & cook about 5 minutes. Be careful not to over cook shrimp.

SERVING SUGGESTIONS:

Serve with a salad & bread.

Judy Mohler
Indiana Wesleyan Wildcat Challenge
Marion, Indiana

Heaven on a Plate

INGREDIENTS:

1 lb. med. shrimp(peeled & deveined)
1 red pepper
1 green pepper
1 sm. onion
3 cloves garlic
10 sliced mushrooms
olive oil
2 lemons
parsley
crushed red pepper-optional (if you like it hot)
1 lb. angel hair pasta

DIRECTIONS:

Sauté garlic, onions, peppers and mushrooms in olive oil (enough to coat large frying pan). Simmer for 10 minutes. Add juice of 2 lemons. Add shrimp for 5 minutes. Boil water for angel hair pasta.

SERVING SUGGESTIONS:

Serve over angel hair pasta with fresh lemon, and grated romano cheese with a small salad and Italian bread. Enjoy!

Marc Ingellis
Boca Raton Road Runners
Boca Raton, Florida

"Down the Bayou"

INGREDIENTS:

2 cans Cream of Shrimp soup
1 can Cream of Mushroom soup
4 cups seafood: shrimp, scallops & crab
dash salt & pepper
1 tsp. curry powder
2 stalks chopped celery
1/2 chopped green pepper
1 lrg. diced onion
1-12 oz. pkg. fresh mushrooms

DIRECTIONS:

Sauté all chopped vegetables in olive oil. In a large pot combine all soups & spices. Add in sautéed vegetables & simmer. Sauté all seafood until tender - not too long or seafood gets rubbery. Add seafood to soup pot & simmer on low with lid off. Serve over hot, white fluffy rice.

SERVING SUGGESTIONS:

"Down the Bayou" can be easily doubled in a large pot to serve to a big crowd. Accompany with a salad & crusty loaf of french bread for a simple, crowd pleasing meal.

Maureen Middleton
Metroplex Hospital Silver Classic 5K
Harker Heights, Texas

Citrus Salmon Bake

INGREDIENTS:

1 1/2 lb. salmon filets or other fish
1 med. chopped onion
salt & pepper to taste
3 tblsp. chopped dill weed
4 tsp. oil
2 tsp. grated orange rind
2 tsp. grated lemon rind
orange & lemon slices

DIRECTIONS:

Place oil and chopped onion in bottom of crockpot (or baking dish). Salt & pepper fish to taste, and place it on top. Sprinkle grated peel and dill weed over fish. Cook on low for 1 1/2 hours or in the oven @ 450° for 10 minutes per inch of thickness.

SERVING SUGGESTIONS:

Serve with wild and brown rice pilaf and steamed broccoli.

Laurie Arizumi
Tuscaloosa Track Club
Tuscaloosa, Alabama

Portland Marathon Clam Chowder

INGREDIENTS:

1/2 lb. thinly sliced bacon
1 med. chopped carrot
1 can drained shrimp
1/2 tblsp. salt
1 sm. chopped yellow onion
3 cans drained & chopped clams
3/4 cups flour
1 med. diced rib of celery
3/4 cup butter (+ 1 tblsp.)
1/2 cup clam juice
1 tblsp. dried basil
5 cloves garlic
1 qt. half &half
1/2 tsp. pepper

DIRECTIONS:

Cut all of fat off bacon (use lean meat). Sauté bacon with 2 tblsp. butter, celery, onion, carrot & garlic in a large soup pot over medium heat for 5 minutes. Reduce heat to medium-low and stir in the clam juice, half & half, clams & seasonings. Blend remaining butter in sauce pan with flour until smooth. Stir constantly & cook 1 minute. Add mixture & vegetables in pot & stir until it thickens. Do not boil! Stir in shrimp at the last & serve as soon as they are heated. Sauté vegetables until tender crisp. Serve immediately, after adding the flour, butter & shrimp so vegetables remain crisp.

Les Smith
Portland Marathon
Portland, Oregon

Cajun Pasta

I N G R E D I E N T S :

2 tblsp. butter
2 tblsp. green onions
cajun spice mix
2 oz. diced ham
3-4 shrimp
1 oz. crab meat
6 oz. cooked spaghetti
1 cup cream

D I R E C T I O N S :

Cube ham into 1/4" squares and toss with plenty of cajun spice mix. Let stand at least 1 hour. Heat butter in skillet. Add green onions and ham. Saute 1-2 minutes. Add shrimp, cook until just done (do not over cook). Add crab meat, cream and sprinkle with more cajun spice mix. Cook until cream reduces into a thick sauce. Toss with hot spaghetti and serve immediately. May double, triple ingredients as desired.

S E R V I N G   S U G G E S T I O N S :

Serve with small green tossed salad and French bread, and don't forget the red wine of your choice.

Diane Lahr
Mississippi Valley Running Club
Dubuque, Iowa

Greek Shrimp Over Rice

INGREDIENTS:

1 lb. fresh shrimp
about 2 cups each of the following;
    white seedless grapes
    diced celery
    diced green pepper
    diced sweet onion
1 1/2 cups rice
1/2 stick of butter
1 tsp. salt
1 tblsp. Old Bay seasoning
1-2 tblsp. Zeus seasoning or other Greek seasoning

DIRECTIONS:

Peel, devein and rinse shrimp. Massage in Old Bay or your favorite seafood seasoning and set aside. Mix equal amounts of grapes, onion, celery, and green pepper with Greek seasoning in a large skillet with just enough water to cover the bottom. Place shrimp on top of the vegetables and steam on high for about 8-10 minutes. Serve over rice and eat while it is still steaming.
To cook rice: Bring 3 cups of water to a boil. Add the juice of 1/2 lemon, salt, butter and rice. Bring to a second boil. Cover tightly and simmer on low for about 20-25 minutes. Do not stir or open cover.

SERVING SUGGESTIONS:

You may add black olives and mushrooms for additional flavor and color. However, this is best when you keep it simple.

Charles McCormick
Wilmington Road Runners
Wilmington, North Carolina

Seafood Chowder

INGREDIENTS:

1/2 lb. peeled & deveined shrimp (fresh)
1/2 lb. bay scallops (rinsed)
2 med. peeled & cubed potatoes
1 tblsp. butter
1 med. diced tomato
1 med. diced onion
1 can chicken broth
1 can Cream of Celery Soup (Healthy Choice)
1 tblsp. Old Bay seasoning
fresh chopped parsley

DIRECTIONS:

Lightly sauté onions & tomato in butter, using medium saucepan. Add chicken broth & potatoes. Cook until tender. Do not over cook! Add shrimp, scallops & Old Bay. Cook just until seafood is done (about 3 minutes). Add cream of celery soup & stir gently. Garnish with parsley.

Serves 2 hungry people!

SERVING SUGGESTIONS:

This chowder is great with a hot sourdough roll.

Jeanie McCormick
Wilmington Road Runners
Wilmington, North Carolina

Baked Alaska King Salmon

INGREDIENTS:

1 or 2 lrg. King Salmon fillets
1/2 bottle Kickoman Teriyaki baste and glaze
1/2 cube butter
crushed garlic
salt
pepper
parsley
onion-cut into rings

DIRECTIONS:

Melt butter, crushed garlic and teriyaki baste and glaze then pour over fish. (Use a pan that has no rack). Salt and pepper fish, add onion rings and parsley. Cover with foil. Preheat oven to 450° and cook for 40 minutes. Uncover last 5 minutes, making sure there is no drippings on the bottom of the pan so it won't burn.

Serves 6

SERVING SUGGESTIONS:

The best King Salmon is caught in the Copper River Delta at Cordova, Alaska in May or June. The fish are at their prime in these times because they are ready to spawn which makes them full of fat. This fat contains omega 3 and makes the fish very rich, Always rinse your fish in cold water a few times before cooking.

Irene Webber
Alaska Salmon Runs
Cordova, Alaska

Skillet Shrimp & Sausage

INGREDIENTS:

1 tblsp. olive oil
1 lrg. chopped shallot
2 cloves minced garlic
1/2 lb. mild smoked sausage sliced thick
3/4 lb. peeled and deveined shrimp
1/3 cup white wine
1 tblsp. dried rosemary
1 tsp. dried thyme
1/2 tsp. dried oregano
pinch of crushed red pepper flakes (optional)

DIRECTIONS:

Heat olive oil in medium non-stick skillet over medium high heat. Sauté shallot and garlic 1-2 minutes until lightly browned. Add sausage to skillet and cook 2 more minutes. Add shrimp to the skillet, then pour in wine. Cook 2-3 minutes or until most of the liquid is gone. Stir in seasonings, add salt and pepper to taste and lower the heat. Stir one minute longer to allow flavor to blend.

SERVING SUGGESTIONS:

Serve immediately over fettuccine or linguine-type pasta. Recipe can be easily doubled.

Lee Ann Riloff
Sesame Place Classic
Ambler, Pennsylvania

MJ's Clam Chowder

INGREDIENTS:

3 cans minced clams
1/4 lb. turkey bacon
4 cups diced, peeled potatoes
1/4 cup chopped onion
3 cups 2% milk
3 tblsp. flour
1 tsp. salt
1 1/2 cup water

DIRECTIONS:

Fry bacon till crisp, set aside. In same pan, add onions, potatoes, liquid from the can minced clams and 1 1/2 cup water. Cook till potatoes are tender, about 20 minutes. Add clams and 2 cups milk. In separate bowl mix remaining 1 cup milk with flour, then add slowly to soup mixture and cook till boiling. Add salt, pepper to taste then stir in the bacon. Serve hot.

SERVING SUGGESTIONS:

Great with warm rolls and tossed salad.

Larry Jablonski
Urbandale Track Club Capital Striders
Urbandale, Iowa

Crawfish Etoufée

INGREDIENTS:

1/4 cup corn oil
1 cup chopped onion
1 cup chopped green pepper
1/4 cup fresh chopped parsley
1 tsp. garlic powder
1 tsp. cayenne pepper
1 tsp. cornstarch
2 lbs. peeled crawfish tails or shrimp, deveined and washed
1 1/2 to 2 cups water
1 can Cream of Mushroom Soup

DIRECTIONS:

Sauté chopped vegetables in oil until tender. Stir in seasonings. Blend cornstarch with approximately 1/4 cup water. Slowly stir into skillet mixture. Add Cream of Mushroom Soup. Add crawfish tails or shrimp and gradually stir in 1 cup water. Simmer for 15-20 minutes stirring occasionally. Add more water as needed for desired consistency.

SERVING SUGGESTIONS:

Serve over hot steamed rice.

Charles Lancon
Cajun Roadrunners
Breaux Bridge, Louisiana

Nantucket Bay Scallops In The Pasta Shell

INGREDIENTS:

10-12 fresh peeled plum tomatoes or 2 lbs. of canned tomatoes
1 1/2 lb. bay scallops
1 med. onion
2 cloves garlic
hot pepper (optional)
fresh parsley or basil
2-3 splashes heavy cream
1 lb. pasta shells
salt
herb paste (optional)

DIRECTIONS:

Let tomatoes melt in a saucepan over medium-high flame. Chop onions & add to tomatoes. Add 1 or more hot peppers (your call). Add scallops. Let simmer. Have boiled water ready for pasta. While pasta cooks, prepare parsley, basil & garlic by cutting & blending together until it's a loose paste. Drain pasta well. Put 1/2 of pasta into a warmed serving dish. Pour tomato sauce over the top. Add the splashes of cream. Add the rest of the pasta. Top with herb paste & toss all ingredients together quickly. Serve with grated Parmesan cheese.

Serve 4

Hector MacDonald
Fingerprints Corp.
Charlotte, North Carolina

Wrightwood Smoked Salmon

INGREDIENTS:

1 cup maple syrup
1 cup water
3 tblsp. salt
1-12"-16" salmon
1 charcoal barbeque
15 charcoal briquettes
30 hardwood sticks approximately 8"long x 1"diameter
cherry, apple or pear (something similar)
1 pail of water

DIRECTIONS:

Mix the maple syrup, water, & salt. Warm to dissolve the salt. Filet the salmon. Place the filets in the syrup mixture and refrigerate overnight. Soak the hardwood in the pail of water overnight. When ready to cook, light the charcoal and let it burn for about 45 minutes. Add enough wet hardwood to create a good smoke when the lid is put on the barbeque. Regulate the air that gets to the fire so it smokes, but has little flame. Place the salmon, skin side down, on the barbeque, and put the lid on. Baste with the remaining syrup mixture periodically. Use it all. Smoke until cooked, 2-4 hours, depending on the heat of the fire.

SERVING SUGGESTIONS:

The smoked salmon may be divided, frozen in freezer bags, and thawed in the microwave. It can be served with crackers and cream cheese as an appetizer, on a bagel with cream cheese, or crumbled in a salad with parmesan or feta cheese.

Kathy Smith
Wrightwood Mountain
Wrightwood, California

Fish Creole

I N G R E D I E N T S :

1 lb. flounder fillets
2 tblsp. margarine
1/4 cup chopped onion
1/4 lb. sliced mushrooms
1/4 cup chopped green pepper
1 can drained & chopped tomatoes
2 tblsp. lemon juice
1/4 tsp. dried tarragon
1 bay leaf
1/4 tsp. Tabasco
2 cups cooked rice
salt & pepper to taste

D I R E C T I O N S :

Melt margarine in skillet, add onion & green pepper. Cook for about 5-8 minutes or until just barley tender. Add mushrooms and cook 3 minutes longer. Add tomatoes, lemon juice, tarragon, bay leaf & Tabasco. Cover and simmer for 20 minutes. Remove bay leaf and salt and pepper to taste. Add flounder and simmer, covered for 5-10 minutes, or until fish flakes with a fork.

S E R V I N G   S U G G E S T I O N S :

Serve over steamed rice

Charles Lancon
Cajun Roadrunners
Breaux Bridge, Louisiana

Seafood Pasta

INGREDIENTS:

1 lb. scallops, shrimp (or 1/2 each)
2 tblsp. butter or margarine
1 tblsp. olive oil
1 cup dry, white wine
1 tsp. crushed dried basil
2 med. (1 cup) chopped tomatoes
1/4 cup grated parmesan cheese
1/2 cup snipped parsley
1 lb. pasta

DIRECTIONS:

In saucepan melt 2 tablespoons margarine, add olive oil. Stir in wine, basil, 1/2 teaspoon salt, and 1/8 teaspoon pepper. Bring to a boil, then reduce heat. Boil gently uncovered for 12-15 minutes or until 2/3 of the liquid is evaporated. Add seafood, cover and simmer for about 5 minutes or until scallops are just tender. Stir in chopped tomatoes and heat through. Toss pasta with 1/4 cup melted margarine. Add seafood mix, cheese and parsley. Toss until pasta is coated.

Serves 4

Kelly Colby
Nathan Littauer Hospital
Gloversville, New York

52 Chicken Pick Up

Grilled Walnut Chicken with Wild Rice & Orzo

Fast Running Chinese Chicken Legs

Mustard Roasted Chicken

Mule Mountain Chicken and Rice

Chicken Breast with Spicy Tarragon Brown Rice

Chicken "Popeye" Potpie

Bulldog Salsa Chicken

Not Alot in the Cabinet

Yum Yum Chicken

Hawaiian Style Nasi Goreng

No Guilt Chicken Pot Pie

Chicken Ginger with Carrots & Fruit

Cornish Game Hen LaOrange

Chicken Caciatore

Chicken D. Lite

Myers Favorite Chicken Stir Fry

Chicken Satay & Peanut Sauce

Quick Mexican Chicken and Rice

Southwestern Burritos

Poulet d'Artichoke

Grilled Walnut Chicken with Wild Rice & Orzo

INGREDIENTS:

1 chicken breast for each person
walnut marinade
wild rice - orzo with toasted walnuts

Walnut marinade:
1/4 cup walnut oil
1/4 cup corn, safflower, or peanut oil
1/4 cup white wine vinegar
2 tblsp. chopped fresh basil, or 2 tsp dried
1/2 cup coarsely chopped walnuts
freshly ground pepper

DIRECTIONS:

Combine all the ingredients for marinade in a bowl. Whisk to emulsify. Marinade chicken breasts over night. Grill chicken 6-7 minutes each side. Prepare wild rice (can be made a day ahead of time). Slice chicken breasts into 1/4" wide strips & serve over wild rice & orzo. Can be served at room temperature.

SERVING SUGGESTIONS:

Serve with a simple tossed greens salad, hard rolls and a choice of roasted vegetables.

Betsy Titterington
Mid America Running Association
Trinity Hospital Hill Run
Kansas City, Missouri

Fast Running
Chinese Chicken Legs

INGREDIENTS:

1 dz. chicken legs or thighs
Teriyaki sauce
1 tsp. garlic powder
1/2 tsp. ginger (or about 12 ginger slices from jar)
peanut oil
sesame seeds (about 1/4 -1/2 cup)
1/8 cup sherry to marinade (optional)

DIRECTIONS:

Marinate skinned chicken all day by filling pan with sauce and turn chicken legs once. Place in oven and set oven @ 350°. Sprinkle tops with sesame seeds and bake 1 hour. Serve with rice.

SERVING SUGGESTIONS:

I use either rice or Cous Cous as a starch and stir fry baby corn, mushrooms and sliced water chestnuts, etc. as a vegetable (with a little soy sauce).

Doris Cohen
Schroon Lake Marathon Committee
Schroon Lake, New York

Mustard Roasted Chicken

INGREDIENTS:

1/2 cup dijon mustard
2 tsp. chopped fresh parsley
1 lb. boneless chicken breast
paprika

DIRECTIONS:

Combine mustard and parsley. Arrange chicken pieces in shallow baking pan sprayed with cooking oil. Brush with mustard mixture. Sprinkle evenly with paprika. You can either cook chicken on the grill or bake @ 400° for 45 minutes or until cooked.

Cornelia Montanaro
Lyme Old Lyme P.T.O. - "Trek for Tech"
Old Lyme, Connecticut

Mule Mountain Chicken and Rice

INGREDIENTS:

4 chicken breast
1 cup Saffron rice
3 tblsp. parsley
2 cloves garlic
1 cube vegetable stock
1/4 cup white wine (dry)
1 tblsp. butter
almonds, mozzarella cheese
Salad:
1 bunch spinach
2 tomatoes
3 tblsp. balsamic vinegar
1 tsp. canola oil

DIRECTIONS

Prepare Saffron rice in vegetable stock. Pressure cook chicken with skin for 20 minutes. Remove skin, cut into 1/4" cubes & fry in olive oil, wine, garlic & butter until slightly over cooked and crunchy. Mix with rice.

SERVING SUGGESTIONS:

Serve on dish with grated almonds on top & sprinkle with mozzarella cheese. Serve with salad and white wine. Rinse leaves and cut up tomatoes. Mix with oil & vinegar.

Leslie Woods
Mule Mountain Marathon
Sierra Vista, Arizona

Chicken Breasts with Spicy Tarragon Brown Rice

INGREDIENTS:

1 cup brown rice
1/4-1/3 cup chopped white onion
1 tsp. crushed garlic
1 can Ro-tel tomatoes
1/4 tsp. tarragon
3/4 cup chicken broth
spray oil
2 lrg. bone-in chicken breasts, skinned (can use breasts fillets)
1 pkg. fresh sliced mushrooms
warm tortillas

DIRECTIONS:

Spray the bottom of a large pot with oil. Add rice, chopped onion, garlic, chicken broth, Ro-tels & tarragon. Heat to a boil, cover and simmer on low to medium heat. Skin chicken breasts, cover with waxed paper and pre-cook in microwave on medium for 6 minutes, turning once half-way through. (skip this step if using fillets). Add mushrooms, chicken & another pinch of tarragon to rice pot. Cover and simmer for 35 minutes more or until liquid is absorbed.

Serves 2 very hungry people (can easily serve 4 civilized folk).

SERVING SUGGESTIONS:

Remove chicken from the bone, cut into bite size pieces. Place rice and chicken onto warm tortillas, roll up and dig in.

Beth W. Lemoine
Club South Runners
Baton Rouge, Louisiana

Chicken "Popeye" Potpie

This is a traditional potpie recipe with a few of our favorite ingredients added!

INGREDIENTS:

1 1/2 tsp. olive oil
2 skinless/boneless chicken breasts chopped in 1" pieces
1 cup coarsely chopped onion
1 clove minced garlic
4 cups rinsed, whole leaf spinach, tightly packed
1 med. size potato boiled, peeled and chopped
1-10.75 oz. can low fat Cream of Mushroom Soup
2 puffed pastry sheets, 17.5 oz. pkg. (Pepperidge Farm)
1/8 tsp. Thyme
Salt & pepper to taste

DIRECTIONS:

Preheat oven to 400°. Thaw 2 sheets of puffed pastry. Grease quiche pan or 10" pie plate. Place one sheet of pastry on bottom of prepared dish. Mold to fit dish. Cut second sheet into 1" strips for top of pie. In large pan, sauté chicken in olive oil until cooked through. Add onion & garlic and sauté until tender. Add mushrooms and sauté 2-3 minutes. Add spinach and cover until wilted. Add potatoes & soup and stir. Pour mixture evenly into prepared baking dish. Place pastry strips across the top in a criss cross fashion. Bake for 40 minutes or until crust is golden brown. Let cool for 5 minutes.

Brian & Dana Maurer
Lincoln Park Pacers
Avon, Colorado

Bulldog Salsa Chicken

INGREDIENTS:

1 cut up fryer chicken
1 bottle hot or mild salsa
1 onion
1 pepper
dash salt & pepper
dash garlic salt
dash cilantro
shredded cheddar or jack cheese

DIRECTIONS:

Preheat oven to 350°. Spray pan with non-fat cooking spray. Place chicken in and sprinkle on dry ingredients. Spoon salsa over chicken & ingredients. Place foil over pan and bake in 350° for one hour. Take out of the oven and remove the foil. Spread more salsa & cheese over top and bake 15-20 minutes more until chicken is done.

SERVING SUGGESTIONS:

Serve with warm flour tortillas and top off with some spanish rice and sangria. Enjoy!

Linda J. Richards
Bradley Bulldog Fun Run
Bradley, California

"Not Alot in the Cabinet"

INGREDIENTS:

1/4 butter
1 box Rice-A-Roni(long grain)
wild rice original - prepared
1 cup chopped onion
4 skinless-boneless chicken breasts, cut in strips
1 tsp. garlic pepper
1 tsp. meat tenderizer
1 tsp. season all
1-14 oz. can drained mushrooms
2 cups chopped broccoli tips

DIRECTIONS:

Prepare rice and set aside. Sauté butter and onions in iron skillet. Add chicken and seasonings until chicken is tender. Add broccoli & mushrooms. When broccoli is slightly tender add rice and let set for about 5 minutes.

SERVING SUGGESTIONS:

Serve with hot buttered flour tortillas topped with garlic salt.

Laura Pollard
Habitat for Humanity
Victoria, Texas

Yum Yum Chicken

INGREDIENTS:

1 chicken - cooked, boned & meat chopped
1 can Cream of Celery Soup
1 can Cream of Chicken Soup
1 cup (8 oz.) sour cream
1/2 cup chicken broth
1 box Stove Top Stuffing Mix(Cornbread style)
1 stick butter

DIRECTIONS:

Spray casserole dish with Pam. Place chopped chicken in bottom of a
9"x13" casserole. Combine soups and sour cream and spread over chicken.
Remove stuffing mix, bread packet & seasoning packet from box-empty
these in a mini food processor until you have fine crumbs. Place these on
top of soup mixture. Top this with melted butter & chicken broth that have
been mixed together. Cook for 55 minutes @ 350°. Tastes like chicken &
dressing.

Charles Whitaker
Audie Murphy Hero Run
Farmersville, Texas

Hawaiian Style Nasi Goreng

INGREDIENTS:

5 boneless, skinless cubed chicken breasts
1 cup cubed Kalua Pig or cooked ham
1 bunch chopped Pak Choy or leek
3 cups cooked rice
2 chopped onions
1 clove minced garlic
3 tsp. cooking oil or olive oil
1 bay leaf
1 sprig parsley
1/2 tsp. salt
1 tsp. coriander
1 tsp. cumin
1/4 tsp. crushed chili pepper
1/8 tsp. mace
1 egg
1/2 cup pineapple
2 tblsp. peanut butter (chunky)
Sambel Oelak (Indonesian chili paste) to taste

DIRECTIONS:

Cook rice and hold aside. Cook chicken and pig with ham along with Pak Choy or leek until tender. In oil, cook onions until soft. Add garlic & meat/vegetable mix. Add spices and peanut butter. Break an egg over mixture and scramble until done. Add pineapple. Add rice. Mix and serve.

SERVING SUGGESTIONS:

As condiments, sere with chopped peanuts. Add Sambol Oelek to taste.

Marilyn L. Nicholson
Kilauea Volcano Wilderness and Rim Runs
Hawaii National Park, Hawaii

No Guilt Chicken Pot Pie

INGREDIENTS:

1-10 3/4 oz. Campell's condensed 98% fat free Cream of Chicken Soup
1-9 oz. pkg. frozen mixed vegetables, thawed
1 cup cubed cooked chicken
1/2 cup 2% milk
1 cup Bisquick Reduced Fat Baking Mix
1 egg

DIRECTIONS:

Preheat oven to 400°. In 9" pie plate mix soup, vegetables & chicken. Mix milk, egg, & baking mix. Pour over chicken mixture. Bake 30 minutes or until golden brown.

SERVING SUGGESTIONS:

Prep time is 10 minutes. Cook time is 30 minutes.

Lee Ann Aurandt
YMCA
Johnstown, Pennsylvania

Ginger Chicken with Carrots & Fruit

INGREDIENTS:

6 boneless skinless chicken breasts cut into 1 1/2" strips
3 tsp. ground ginger
1/4 cup low sodium soy sauce
1 1/2 cups sliced carrots cooked until tender
1 cup pineapple tidbits drained
1 cup frozen tart red cherries
2 tblsp lime juice
1/2 tsp. black pepper
3 cups hot cooked wild rice

DIRECTIONS:

In a small bowl sprinkle chicken strips with 1/2 teaspoon ginger. Stir in soy sauce and let stand for about 10 minutes. In a medium bowl combine carrots, pineapple, cherries, lemon juice, remaining ginger & pepper.
Add chicken strips to sauce and mix well. Place in a shallow 1 quart baking dish. Cook @ 400° for 30 minutes. Serve over wild rice.

Serves 6

Executive Chef Richard Robinson
Provena Saint Joseph Medical Center Racing Hearts
Joliet, Illinois

Cornish Game Hen La Orange

INGREDIENTS:

2 cornish game hens
orange juice
orange marmalade
1/2 box white rice

DIRECTIONS:

Pre-heat oven to 400-450° and wash hens. Place orange marmalade all over hens. Put hens in 2" deep pan then put in oven. From time to time during cooking pour orange juice over hens. Do this several times during cooking. Cook till golden brown (perhaps 2 hour cooking time) or until you are satisfied with the color of hens.

SERVING SUGGESTIONS:

Serve on large platter of rice pilaf placing hen in center. Serve with mint jelly as a tangy taste.

Rick Cagle
Northwest Runners
Seattle, Washington

Chicken Cacciatore

INGREDIENTS:

3 lbs. chicken pieces or 2 lbs. chicken breasts
1/8 cup oil
1 cup finely chopped onion
3/4 cup chopped celery
1 clove minced garlic
2-8 oz. cans tomato sauce
1/2 cup water
1/2 tsp. salt
1/4 tsp. pepper
1/2 tsp. basil

DIRECTIONS:

In skillet brown chicken in oil. Remove and reserve. To skillet add onion, celery & garlic. Cook lightly. Return chicken to skillet along with sauce, water, salt, pepper & basil. Simmer, uncovered, 30-40 minutes.

Makes 4-6 servings

SERVING SUGGESTIONS:

Nice served with spaghetti, green salad, and garlic bread.

> *David W. Jantzen, Jr.*
> Spring Brach Memorial Track Club
> Houston, Texas

Chicken D. Lite

INGREDIENTS:

2 tblsp. olive oil
3 lbs. skinless, bone in or boneless chicken breasts
1 cup white wine, either Semillon or Sauvignon Blanc
1 1/2 cup chicken stock/bouillon
4 med. potatoes sliced 1/2" thick
4 med. carrots cut to 1" inch lengths
2 med. thickly sliced onions
1 tsp. rosemary - fresh is the best but dried works well also

DIRECTIONS:

Heat oil in large skillet. Brown chicken approximately 15 minutes. Add wine & chicken stock/bouillon. Add vegetables. Sprinkle rosemary & chopped garlic over ingredients. Cover & bring to a simmer. Go run for approximately 40 minutes. Cool down, stretch, shower for approximately 20 minutes. Total cooking time is 1 hour 15 minutes.

SERVING SUGGESTIONS:

Thicken remaining liquid with cornstarch. Garnish each plate with sprigs of fresh rosemary. Serve with warm biscuits & the remaining wine of course.

Larry "Cat" Catallo
Hudson Mohawk Road Runners
Waterford, New York

Myers Favorite Chicken Stir Fry

INGREDIENTS:

2 1/3 tblsp. cooking oil (peanut preferred)
3 tblsp. divided soy sauce
2 1/3 tblsp. divided corn starch
1 1/2-2 lbs. boneless, skinned chicken breasts-cut into 1" cubes
1 cup chicken broth (chicken bouillon dissolved in hot water is fine)
1/2 tsp. ground ginger
1/2 tsp. crushed red pepper
1 lrg. onion-cut into 1" pieces
2 cloves minced garlic
1 lrg. bunch fresh broccoli-cut into florettes & 1" stem pieces
3 lrg. peeled carrots-cut into 1/4" rounds
3 stalks celery-cut into 1/2" chevrons

DIRECTIONS:

Mix 1 teaspoon oil, 1 tablespoon soy sauce and 1 teaspoon corn starch in small mixing bowl. Add chicken pieces, mix to coat. Cover & refrigerate while preparing remainder of recipe. Mix chicken broth, ginger, 2 tablespoons soy sauce with 2 tablespoons corn starch in small bowl. Set aside. Chop all vegetables as required. Heat 2 tablespoons oil in large skillet or wok. Add chilled chicken pieces. Sprinkle in red pepper. Stir-fry over medium high heat until chicken is no longer pink. Remove chicken from skillet; set aside. Stir-fry onion & garlic 2-3 minutes or until onion is tender. Add broccoli, carrots & celery, stir-fry until tender. Return chicken to skillet; add chicken broth mixture. Cook, stirring constantly until thickened. Serve with rice.

Serves 4-6

SERVING SUGGESTIONS:

Cook brown rice according to package directions. Serve stir-fry over cooked rice, with added soy sauce. Try green beans, water chestnuts, shredded cabbage, snow peas, be creative!

Cathy Myers
Dayspring Christian Academy
New Providence, Pennsylvania

Chicken Satay & Peanut Sauce

INGREDIENTS:

2 lbs. chicken breasts - cut in 1" strips
3 slices crushed ginger
3 cloves crushed garlic
1 tblsp. curry powder
1 tsp. salt
2 tblsp. butter
1/2 cup coconut milk
satay sticks
Peanut sauce:
1 tblsp. red curry paste
1 tblsp. roasted curry paste
1 tbslp. sugar
2 tbslp. peanut butter
2 cups coconut milk
1 tsp. lemon juice or tamarind juice
1 tsp. salt

DIRECTIONS:

Mix all of the first group of ingredients except chicken. Next add chicken
and marinate at least 2 hours. Thread a few pieces of chicken on the top half
of each satay stick. Can cook over charcoal or broil in oven, turning once.
Stir fry curry pastes together. Add coconut milk, bring to boil. Add the rest
of the ingredients. Serve with peanut sauce.

SERVING SUGGESTIONS:

While living in a small village in Northern Thailand we always had Chicken
Satay when we had quests. It was served with fresh fruit salad and steamed
white rice. In restaurants in Thailand it is usually served with cucumber
salad.

Alice A. Samuelson
Alaska Run for Women
Anchorage, Alaska

Quick Mexican Chicken & Rice

INGREDIENTS:

3-4 skinless, boneless chicken breasts cut into strips
1 tblsp. oil
1/2 cup med. chopped onion
1 clove minced garlic
1-14 1/2 oz. mexican style stewed tomatoes
1 1/4 water or chicken broth
1/2 tsp. chili powder
1 3/4 cup instant brown rice
1/2 cup shredded low-fat cheese (optional)
several dashes of hot pepper sauce (optional)

DIRECTIONS:

In a large skillet brown chicken in hot oil until lightly browned. Remove chicken and set aside. Cook onion & garlic until tender. Add cooked chicken, tomatoes, water or chicken broth, chili powder & hot sauce. Bring to a boil. Add rice, lower heat and cover. Simmer 5 minutes. Remove form the heat. Sprinkle with cheese if desired. Let stand 5 minutes before serving.

Serves 4

SERVING SUGGESTIONS:

We first tried this recipe years ago after seeing it in the Cedar Valley Running Club newsletter and since then it has been a family favorite! It is healthy, lowfat & quick.

George Karr
Regina Fall Fun Run
Iowa City, Iowa

Southwestern Burritos

INGREDIENTS:

10 oz. frozen kernel corn
2 tblsp. corn oil
1-16 oz. can black beans, drained
1 cup chopped green bell pepper
1 cup chopped red onions
2 tblsp. fresh lime juice
3 lrg. pressed garlic cloves
2 oz. canned diced mild green
  chilies
2 tblsp. freshly chopped cilantro
1 tsp. chili powder

10 oz. shredded Monterey Jack
  Cheese
2 lbs. deboned skinless chicken
  breasts
1 pkg. McCormick Southwestern
  Marinade
3 tblsp. corn oil
3 tsp. water
1 tblsp. white vinegar
16 flour tortillas, fajita size
8 oz. guacamole
8 oz. light cream

DIRECTIONS:

Combine marinade mix with vinegar, 3 teaspoons corn oil & water. Stir
well and add chicken. Marinate for 30 minutes. Bake chicken @ 350° for
30 minutes. Let cool. Cut into strips. Combine 3 tablespoons corn oil with
frozen corn in pan. Sauté for 3 minutes. Transfer to large bowl. To corn,
add black beans, bell pepper, red onion, lime juice, garlic, chilies, cilantro,
chili powder and shredded cheese. Toss well. Roll burritos: place a tortilla
shell down, fill with 3 tablespoons of bean mixture. Top with 2-3 strips of
chicken, fold up end closest to you, then fold each side in. Roll over.
Continue until all burritos are rolled. Place burritos seams down in a vegetable sprayed baking dish. Bake @ 350° for 40 minutes. Serve each bur-
rito with 1 ounce of avocado cream sauce and/or sour cream, guacamole,
shredded lettuce, chopped tomatoes.

Avocado Cream Sauce: Combine guacamole and light cream in a sauce
pan. Heat over medium heat while stirring. Whisk until heated through.

Serves 16

Sue Briars
Annapolis Striders
Gambrills, Maryland

Poulet d' Artichoke

INGREDIENTS:

2 cans artichoke hearts
3-4 cups cooked chicken
1 1/2 cans Cream of Chicken Soup
3/4 cups mayonnaise
1 tsp. lemon juice
2 cloves garlic
1/2-1 tsp. curry powder
1 1/4 cup grated sharp cheddar cheese

DIRECTIONS:

Cook artichokes with garlic cloves for 5 minutes. Cut each into 2 and layer in greased oblong baking dish. Add chicken cut into bite size pieces. Combine soup, mayonnaise, lemon juice and curry. Pour over chicken. Sprinkle on cheese. Bake @ 350° for 25 minutes.

SERVING SUGGESTIONS:

Can use low fat soup, mayo & cheese in recipe. Serve with salad, broccoli & sherbet.

Gwen Eckelman
St. Louis Track Club
St. Louis, Missouri

Mostly Vegetarian

Mostly Vegetarian

High Sierra Vegetarian Beans

Mo's Mabu Dofu

Calico Beans

Deb's Cowboy Beans

Cheese Enchilada

Black Bean Enchilada

Eggplant Parmigiana

Artichoke Frittata

Spicy Rice and Beans

Mexican Polenta

Bean Casserole

Turbo Bean Bake

Chimpy's Favorite Eggplant

High Sierra Vegetarian Beans

INGREDIENTS:

1 tblsp. chopped garlic
1 chopped onion
1 can great northern white beans
1 can kidney beans
1 can pinto beans
1 can black beans
1 sm. can chopped tomatoes
1 can corn kernels
1 can pitted black olives
1 chopped bunch fresh cilantro
1 tsp. cumin
1 tsp. chili powder
1/4 tsp. Tabasco sauce
1 or 2 crumbled dried red chilies, if desired. (These will add "fire" to the dish)

DIRECTIONS:

Sauté garlic and onions until golden brown. Add canned beans and vegetables. Add chopped cilantro. Add seasonings - add more if desired. (This is a very mild tasting dish). Simmer for 20-30 minutes.

SERVING SUGGESTIONS:

Serve on a bed of taco chips, topped with grated cheddar or jack cheese.

Marie Boyd
Bishop High Sierra 50
Bishop, California

Mo's Mabu Dofu

INGREDIENTS:

1/2 pkg. diced tofu
1 lb. ground turkey sausage
1 diced carrot
1 diced celery
1/2 diced onion
4 diced garlic cloves
1/2 tsp. grated ginger
1 head cabbage or lettuce

DIRECTIONS:

Sauté carrots, celery, onion, garlic & ginger, 5-7 minutes on medium heat. Cook ground turkey sausage and drain fat. Add sautéed ingredients. Add tofu, simmer on low for 5 minutes. Wrap mixture in cabbage or lettuce.

Serves 4-6

Maureen Borba
YMCA
Tacoma, Washington

Calico Beans

INGREDIENTS:

1/2 lb. turkey bacon(diced)
1/2 lb. ground turkey
1/2 cup chopped onion
1 can kidney beans
1 can butter beans
1 can pork & beans
1/2 cup sugar
1/2 cup brown sugar
1 tsp. salt
1 tsp. dry mustard
3 tsp. vinegar
1/2 cup ketchup

DIRECTIONS:

Brown first 3 ingredients in 2 teaspoon extra virgin olive oil. Drain.
Combine with remaining ingredients in casserole dish or slow cooker.
Bake at 350° for 45 minutes, or in a slow cooker for 2-3 hours.

SERVING SUGGESTIONS:

Serve with crusty French bread. This is a long time favorite of our running club!

Joey Falch
Lakes Area Running Club
Burlington, Wisconsin

Deb's Cowboy Beans

INGREDIENTS:

1 lb. hamburger
1 lb. bacon
1 med. chopped onion
2-32 oz. cans pork-n-beans
Sauce:
1 cup ketchup
1 cup brown sugar
2 tsp. dry mustard
4 tsp. vinegar
2 tsp. worcestershire sauce

DIRECTIONS:

Mix sauce ingredients together first. Heat oven to 325°. Brown and drain hamburger. Cook onion & crumble bacon. Chop onion. Mix together with beans and then mix all above with sauce. Cover and bake 2 hours @ 325°.

SERVING SUGGESTIONS:

A great comfort food. Kids love it. Serve with fresh baked bread or cornbread.

Tami Smith
Iowa River Striders
Marshalltown, Iowa

Cheese Enchiladas

INGREDIENTS:

2-3 cloves minced garlic
1 lrg. chopped onion
2 tblsp. olive oil (can substitute vegetable oil)
2 tblsp. flour
2 cups chicken (or vegetable) broth
4 oz. can chopped mild green chilies
2 cups drained & chopped canned tomatoes
12 corn tortillas
4 cups Monterey Jack or cheddar cheese (or a combination)
Garnishes:
1 sliced avocado
1 cup chopped green onion
2 cups sour cream

DIRECTIONS:

Sauté onion & garlic in oil until soft. Stir in flour and cook about 1 minute. Add broth and stir until thickened over medium to medium-high heat. Add chilies & tomatoes - simmer for 10 minutes. Cool slightly. Pureé in blender; in small batches, if necessary. Dip each tortilla in sauce to soften. Put a large spoonful of cheese and a large spoonful of sauce in each tortilla, roll up and place in large flat, ungreased baking pan. Pour remaining sauce over all and bake uncovered @ 350° for 15 minutes. Serve garnished w/avocado, green onion & sour cream. Not fat free, but so delicious!!

Serves 6

SERVING SUGGESTIONS:

Serve with a salad and spoon bread. This recipe is worth the trouble of pureeing the sauce!

Lynn Smith
Shenandoah Valley Track Club
Harrisonburg, Virginia

Black Bean Enchiladas

INGREDIENTS:

4 cups dried black turtle beans (or substitute canned beans)
6 cloves crushed garlic
2 tsp. ground cumin
2 tsp. dried basil
1/2 tsp. dried oregano
salt, pepper & cayenne pepper to taste
juice of 1 lime
2 med. chopped bell peppers (green, red, or yellow or mix)
2 tblsp. olive oil
2-4 oz. cans diced green chilies
1/2 cup tomato puree
1 lb. grated cheddar cheese
1 dz. whole wheat tortillas
sour cream (optional)

DIRECTIONS:

Soak beans overnight, drain off water & cook in fresh water until tender
(approximately 1 1/2 hours). Transfer cooked beans to a large pot with 2
cups of their cooking water. In skillet, sauté garlic, seasonings, lime juice
& bell pepper in olive oil over low heat until peppers are tender. Add sauté
to cooked beans, along with tomato puree & minced green chilies. Cover
and simmer, over low heat for 30 minutes.

SERVING SUGGESTIONS:

This can be served as chili or the ingredients can be put into a tortilla,
wrapped and placed in a baking dish, covered with grated cheese and
baked in the oven at 300° until cheese melts and mixture is thoroughly
heated. Top with sour cream and serve. If served as chili, top with cheese
or sour cream and serve with warm tortillas.

Barbara L. Bodinson
Big Miles of Kansas City
Kansas City, Missouri

Eggplant Parmigiana

INGREDIENTS:

* This is a low fat version of our popular fried Eggplant Parmigiana. It's easy, quick and delicious!

2 med. size eggplants
1-27.75 oz. jar spaghetti sauce
8 oz. low fat shredded mozzarella

DIRECTIONS:

Preheat oven to 350°. Cure the eggplants by slicing them into 1/4" slices. Salt one side of each slice and layer into a stainer. Let "cure" for 30 minutes. Pour 1/3 of the spaghetti sauce into baking dish. Layer 1/3 of eggplant slices over sauce and cover with 1/3 of the cheese. Repeat two more times ending with the cheese. Cover and bake for 45 minutes or until eggplant is tender and cheese is bubbly. Let cool for 5 minutes and serve with hot garlic bread.

Brian & Dana Maurer
Lincoln Park Pacers
Avon, Colorado

Artichoke Frittata

INGREDIENTS:

3 cloves minced garlic
1 bunch (6) chopped green onions
1 tblsp. olive oil
2-7 oz. sm. jars marinated artichoke hearts, broken into small pieces
(drained)
5 eggs, lightly beaten
6 crumbled soda crackers
3-4 drops, Tabasco sauce
1/4 tsp. salt
1/8 tsp. pepper
1 1/2 cups grated cheddar cheese

DIRECTIONS:

Sauté garlic and onion in olive oil for 5 minutes. Mix together with remaining ingredients, making a batter. Pour the batter into a lightly greased 8-inch square baking dish. Bake @ 350° for 25 minutes. Cut into squares.

Serves 6

SERVING SUGGESTIONS:

This recipe is delicious using egg substitute and reduced-fat or fat free cheese too. Can lighten up even more by using olive oil spray (ie. Pam) instead of the tablespoon olive oil. Serve with a crusty bread and salad. This is a healthy, tasty dinner!

Carolyn "Lynn" Robbins
Carolina Godiva Track Club; NC Roadrunners
Durham, North Carolina

Spicy Rice and Beans

INGREDIENTS:

vegetable cooking spray
1 cup chopped onion
1 lrg. chopped & peeled garlic clove
1 seeded and chopped green pepper
1-14 1/2 oz. undrained stewed tomatoes
1 cup chicken broth
1 tblsp. ground cumin
1 tsp. chili powder, or to taste
3/4 cup long grain rice
16 oz. can drained red kidney beans

DIRECTIONS:

Spray a large saucepan with vegetable cooking spray. Add onion, sauté over medium heat for 5 minutes, stirring frequently. Stir in garlic & green pepper. Sauté 2 minutes longer, still stirring frequently. Add stewed tomatoes, broth, cumin & chili powder, bring to boil. Add rice; reduce heat to low, cover and simmer 18 minutes, or until rice is almost heated through.

* Note; you can reduce sodium by draining & rinsing beans.

Patricia L. Fizell
Crim Festival of Races
Flint, Michigan

Mexican Polenta

INGREDIENTS:

Polenta:
3 cups water
1 tsp. salt
1 cup cornmeal
1 tblsp. chopped fresh cilantro OR
1/2 tsp. red pepper flakes (optional)
Topping:
1-15 oz. can drained black beans
1 cup frozen cut corn
1-4.5 oz. can chopped green chilies
1/2 cup finely chopped red onion
4 oz. shredded Monterey Jack cheese
top with ripe sliced tomatoes

DIRECTIONS:

Preheat oven to 350°. Place water and salt in sauce pan and bring to a boil. Whisk in cornmeal & cilantro or pepper flakes (if desired). Continue to whisk until thickened (about 1 minute). Pour polenta in large baking pan (28x18x4 cm) coated with cooking spray. Let polenta cool slightly until firm (about 5 minutes). Top polenta with remaining ingredients finishing with cheese and tomatoes. Place pan in oven and go for a 30-40 minute run. Dinner is ready when you return!

SERVING SUGGESTIONS:

Serve with your favorite salsa. Of course, this recipe can easily be modified to fit whatever you have on hand or whatever you prefer. Topping with green chili sauce or salsa instead of tomatoes works good. To serve carnivores, simply add taco seasoned hamburger and mexican sausage.

Brenda Alexander
High Plains Harriers
Larami, Wyoming

Bean Casserole

INGREDIENTS:

1 cup chopped onion
1/2 cup chopped celery
1 lb. can green beans(drained)
1 lb. can yellow beans(drained)
1 lb. can black beans(drained)
3-1 lb. cans vegetarian baked beans with sauce
1 lb. can fancy red kidney beans(drained)
1 lb. can red chili beans in gravy
1 lb. garbanzo beans(drained)
1/2 cup brown sugar
1 tblsp. mustard
1/2 cup ketchup
fennel seed to taste
Italian seasoning herb blend, to taste

DIRECTIONS:

Combine all ingredients in slow cooker, cook 6-8 hours or overnight.

> *Dee Crowe*
> BBC Striders
> Belleville, Michigan

Turbo Bean Bake

INGREDIENTS:

2 cups kidney beans (1 or 2-16 oz. cans)
1 tblsp. dried basil
1 tblsp. dried oregano
1 bouillon cube
1-15 oz. can tomato sauce
1-8 oz. can tomato paste
1/2 cup low fat Ricotta cheese
6 tortilla, corn or flour
1 cup grated part skim mozzarella cheese
1 chopped onion
1 minced garlic clove
1/8 tsp. pepper
1 tsp. dried parsley

DIRECTIONS:

In a saucepan stir together and heat beans, onion, garlic, seasonings & bouillon cube. Add tomato sauce & paste and cook for 20 minutes, stirring occasionally. Add Ricotta cheese and stir, continue cooking. Line bottom of 11"x7" shallow glass baking dish with 6 tortillas. Spread with bean mixture and then the cheese. Bake uncovered @ 400° for 30 minutes.

Serves 4

SERVING SUGGESTIONS:

Serve with green salad, non-fat ranch dressing and corn muffins.

> *Kristi Mally*
> Cascade Cruisers
> Osceola, Wisconsin

Starving Artist Meatballs

INGREDIENTS:

Italian flavored breadcrumbs
eggs
grated parmesan cheese
olive oil
black or white pepper

* I have never seen my grandmother, nor my mother measure any of the ingredients, so I do it in the same way. So here's how we do it;

DIRECTIONS:

In a dry bowl put approximately 7/8 cup of the breadcrumbs. Break 4 eggs into the breadcrumbs. Prep a frying pan by heating on medium to high heat, pour in olive oil. You are looking for an oatmeal like consistency. This will determine the proper ratio of egg to breadcrumb. Use water to make up the difference instead of adding more eggs. BUT, don't use too much water or they will get soggy. Once you have the proper consistency, sprinkle about 3 teaspoons of grated cheese and a teaspoon of pepper in the mix. Use a large spoon and scoop the mix. Drop into oil that is approximately 1/8 inch thick. Allow them to brown. A little "black" around the edges is fine. After they have cooked (break one open and check the middle, like checking a fat pancake) drop them into your favorite Italian pasta sauce and allow to simmer for at least 45 minutes. Serve with pasta dish. They can replace or assist meatballs.

Robert Liguori
Cindy's Run
Yaphank, New York

Chimpy's Favorite Eggplant

INGREDIENTS:

1 lrg. eggplant
1 sliced red bell pepper
1 med. chopped white onion
2 tblsp. sun-dried tomatoes soaked in olive oil
black pepper, to taste
2 tblsp. grated parmesan cheese
2 tblsp. olive oil

DIRECTIONS:

Slice eggplant in circles. Salt and let sit for 20 minutes. Pat dry. Heat olive oil in stir fry pan. Add onion & bell pepper. Toss in pan to coat evenly with olive oil. Add eggplant. Toss again. Turn heat to medium, cover for 5 minutes to steam lightly. Add black pepper & parmesan. Toss again. Cover, steam for 7-10 minutes.

SERVING SUGGESTIONS:

Add mini-carrots, apples, cucumbers, as side dishes to provide a well-rounded veggie meal. Serve hot with rice. Also great served with pasta.

Lisa Paige
Colorado Columbines Womens Running Club
Littleton, Colorado

Salads &
Side Lines

Salads and Side Lines

Poke Greens

Sauce From Hell

Garlic Goo

30-06 Mustard

Strawberry Jello Salad

Chicken Salad with Greens

Spinach Salad with Chutney Dressing

Race Director's Salvation Salad

Broccoli Salad

Sweet-Sour Stawberry Spinach Salad

Fruit Slaw

Grandpa's Potatoes

Good Rice

Kechnie Korn Kasserole

Sour Cream Potatoes

Rice Casserole

Classic Corn Casserole

Sprinters Sweet Spuds

Mexican Rice Casserole

Gramma Sylvia's Famous Corn Casserole

Turkey Trot Squash Casserole

Cheese and Carrot Casserole

POKE (Poke Greens)

INGREDIENTS:

bucket full Poke
1 tblsp. real butter
1 round onion
salt to taste

DIRECTIONS:

Go find Poke Weed. Look along road sides or waste places. It is probably best to know someone who knows what Poke looks like and have them with you to identify what you have found. Pick poke only in the spring when the leaves are tender and green. CAUTION: Don't eat the Poke berries or roots as they are poisonous. Place fresh Poke in a large pot of water. IMPORTANT: Parboil two times. Bring to boil and then pour off water. Repeat, bring to a boil and pour off water. For the third boil, add butter, onion and salt. Cover and boil until tender. Tastes like fresh spinach. For a variety you can add Turnip greens, Mustard greens, Collards and/or sliced boiled eggs.

Charley Peyton
Arkansas Traveller - 100 Miler
Little Rock, Arkansas

Sauce From Hell

INGREDIENTS:

2 qts. peeled, cored, chopped tomatoes
1 1/2 cup chopped, seeded, long hot red peppers
2 cups vinegar
1 cup sugar
1 tblsp. salt
2 tblsp. mixed pickling spices
1 cup chopped onion
6 cloves garlic

DIRECTIONS:

Use rubber gloves to remove seeds from peppers. Combine tomatoes, peppers, onions & garlic with vinegar. Cook until tomatoes are soft. Press through a sieve or food mill. Add sugar & salt. Put spices in a tea ball and add to tomato mixture. Cook about 30 minutes or until thick. As mixture thickens, stir frequently. Cook until desired thickness, about 20-30 minutes. Pour boiling hot into Ball or Mason Jars , leaving 1/8" head space. Process 10-15 minutes.

Makes about 4 half-pints.

SERVING SUGGESTIONS:

Use with caution. Make sure that plenty of beverages are available!

Richard Matthews
General Butler Off-Road Triathlon
Owenton, Kentucky

Garlic Goo

INGREDIENTS:

2 eggs
1 cup craft parmesan cheese
2 tsp. worcestershire
1/2 cup bottled lemon juice
8 lrg. cloves garlic
1 cup vegetable oil

DIRECTIONS:

Blend first 5 ingredients in a blender. <u>Slowly</u> add oil while blending.
Refrigerate 1 day. Eat on everything!

SERVING SUGGESTIONS:

Great dip for warm sourdough, as a dressing, on meats, fish, chicken, over
baked potatoes, pasta, rice, veggies, etc.!!! Keeps for up to 2 weeks in the
fridge. Also the recipe easily doubles.

Judy R. Alvey & Matt Hanko
Gone Nuts for Newman Run
Newman, California

30-06 Mustard

INGREDIENTS:

4 oz. dry mustard
1/2 cup vinegar
1/2 tsp. salt
1/2 cup beer
1 1/2 tsp. black pepper
1/4 cup sugar

DIRECTIONS:

Mix all ingredients together. Let stand for 48 hours. It is sweet, but very hot. Use sparingly.

SERVING SUGGESTIONS:

Use on ham sandwiches, fried fish or any kind of sandwiches.

Geneva Meadows
Mississippi Valley Running Association
Grand Mound, Louisiana

Strawberry Jello Salad

INGREDIENTS:

2 lrg. boxes strawberry jello
2-10 oz. frozen, sliced strawberries
1 lrg. can crushed pineapple
3 mashed bananas
1/2 cup or more chopped pecans or walnuts
1 lrg. container of sour cream

DIRECTIONS:

Let strawberries thaw. Drain juice from pineapple into measuring cup. Then add enough water to make 2 cups. Put in pan & bring to a boil. Dissolve jello with liquid. Add frozen strawberries, pineapple, mashed bananas & nuts. Ladle 1/2 of mixture to a large flat bowl. When it sets, put sour cream over it. Ladle rest of jello mixture over strawberries & let gel.

Mary Schudy
Missoula Road & Track Club
Missoula, Montana

Chicken Salad with Grapes

INGREDIENTS:

1 cup uncooked wild rice
2 cups cooked, chopped chicken
1 cup drained & chopped water chestnuts
3/4 cup Light mayonnaise
1 cup halved cashews
1 1/2 cup green grapes cut in half
dash of curry (optional)

DIRECTIONS:

Cook rice. Drain & cool. Mix with other ingredients. Serve immediately or chill.

Elaine M. Cornwell
Carpet Capital Running Club
Dalton, Georgia

Spinach Salad & Chutney Dressing

INGREDIENTS:

12-16 oz. washed spinach, torn into bite-size pieces
8 oz. washed & sliced mushrooms
3-4 oz. crumbled feta cheese
1 sliced red onion
1/2 lb. fried & crumbled bacon
1/4 cup red wine vinegar
2 tblsp. chutney
3 cloves crushed garlic
1 tblsp. Dijon mustard
1 tblsp. sugar
1/2 cup canola oil

DIRECTIONS:

Toss salad ingredients in a bowl; set aside. Put all dressing ingredients in a blender and blend until well mixed. Pour over salad just before serving & then toss all ingredients.

SERVING SUGGESTIONS:

This salad makes a wonderful summer meal when served with French bread & a good Sauvignon Blanc or Chardonnay.

Kathy Cooper
Rochelle Run
Rochelle, Illinois

Race Director's Salvation Salad

INGREDIENTS:

16 oz. pkg. cooked mostaccioli
1 1/2 cup vinegar
1 1/2 cup sugar
2 tblsp. Dijon mustard
1 tsp. salt
1 tsp. pepper
1 tblsp. chopped parsley
1 med. sliced onion
1 med. thinly sliced cucumber
2 sliced carrots
1/2 cup celery (optional)
1/2 cup green pepper (optional)
1/2 cup sliced black olives (optional)

DIRECTIONS:

Prepare pasta according to directions and drain. Place onions, cucumbers, carrots & other vegetables with pasta. Place remaining ingredients in blender and blend well. Pour over pasta & vegetables. Refrigerate well. Keeps 2 weeks. Makes 3 quarts. I use a gallon glass jar for storage in the refrigerator.

Mary Jo Greene
Bully Bullhead Run
Ruthuen, Iowa

Broccoli Salad

INGREDIENTS:

2 bunches broccoli florets
1 med. finely diced purple onion
1 cup golden raisins
1 cup grated reduced fat sharp cheddar cheese
Dressing:
1 cup fat free mayonnaise
2 tblsp. cider vinegar
10-12 tsp. sugar

DIRECTIONS:

Add dressing & mix well. Chill 1-2 hours before serving.

SERVING SUGGESTIONS:

This is a great cold side dish.

Kim Rutland
Hattiesburg, Mississippi

Sweet-Sour
Strawberry Spinach Salad

INGREDIENTS:

6-8 cups spinach
1 cup strawberries
1 cup sugar
1 tsp. paprika
1/2 tsp. dry mustard
1 tsp. Worcestershire sauce
1 cup oil
1 tsp. minced onion
1/2 cup white vinegar
1/4 cup poppy seeds
1/4 cup sesame seeds

DIRECTIONS:

Mix together ingredients, but do not add to spinach & strawberries. Serve separately. Mix spinach & strawberries. Pour on liquid mixture to individual taste.

SERVING SUGGESTIONS:

This is a very refreshing salad. Very low in fat!

Karen Raymer
Mid America Running Association
Raymore, Missouri

Fruit Slaw

INGREDIENTS:

2 cups cabbage(shredded finely)
1/4 cup pineapple pieces
1 orange(sectioned out)
1 red apple(chopped)
2 tblsp. nuts(chopped)
1/2 cup yogurt, mayonnaise or combo of both
1/4 cup fruit juice

DIRECTIONS:

Just mix the cabbage and fruit. Combine yogurt with fruit the juice and pour over mixture.

John R. Snyder
Ohio River Road Runners
Ansonia, Ohio

Run for the Kitchen

Grandpa's Potatoes

INGREDIENTS:

1 pkg. frozen hash brown potatoes
1 pt. sour cream
1 1/2 cup grated cheese
1/2 cup melted margarine
1/4 cup sherry
1/2 cup onions
1 can Cream of Chicken Soup
   (or Cream of Mushroom or Celery for Vegetarians)
3 cups crushed corn flakes
1/3 cup melted margarine

DIRECTIONS:

Combine all ingredients in a 9"x13" baking pan. Bake @ 350° for 1/2 hour. Then combine 3 cups crushed cornflakes and 1/3 cup melted butter. Put this mixture on top of casserole and bake for 45 more minutes.

Laura Clark
Saratoga Striders
Saratoga Springs, New York

192

Good Rice

INGREDIENTS:

butter (to taste)
2 oz chopped onion
1 cup rice
3 tblsp. dry white wine
2 cups chicken broth
2 tblsp. grated parmesan cheese

DIRECTIONS:

Melt butter and add onions, let cook over medium heat, for a few minutes.
Add rice, broth & wine. Stir until liquid is absorbed on medium heat. Add
cheese and simmer for a few more minutes.

SERVING SUGGESTIONS:

Good with chicken or wild game birds.

Sam Rice
Indian Creek Run
Tulon, Illinois

Kechnie Korn Kasserole

INGREDIENTS:

1 lrg. chopped onion
2 med. chopped green peppers
1/2 cup margarine
1/4 cup flour
2 cup frozen or fresh corn
2 cups cooked white rice
1-14 1/2 oz. can diced tomatoes
10 oz. shredded cheddar cheese
2 tblsp. tamarin or worcestershire sauce
2-3 tblsp. hot pepper sauce or salsa (mild, med. or hot)

Optional: use mozzarella & garlic cheese, use less margarine and add more salsa, jalapeno peppers, & chop up some hard boiled eggs.

DIRECTIONS:

In a large skillet sauté onions and peppers in margarine till tender. Stir in flour. Take off heat. Add remaining ingredients, except 1/2 cup of cheese. Pour into greased baking dish or a stone dish. Bake uncovered for 45 minutes @ 350°. Top with cheese and let stand.

Serves 6-8

SERVING SUGGESTIONS:

This is a great dish for dinner, picnics or Superbowl Sunday. You can offset this healthy Mexican dish with something off balanced like margaritas or fat laden nachos. Enjoy!

Allyson McKechnie
Pagoda Pacers
Shillington, Pennsylvania

Sour Cream Potatoes

INGREDIENTS:

2 lb. pkg. hashbrown potatoes
1/2 cup melted margarine
1 tsp. salt
1/2 chopped onion
1 can Cream of Chicken Soup
1-8 oz. carton of sour cream
1 can of Cheddar Cheese Soup

DIRECTIONS:

Mix all ingredients except hashbrowns, sour cream & Cheddar Cheese Soup and spread into a 8"x15" casserole dish. Add potatoes. Pour sour cream mixture over potatoes. Spread Cheddar Cheese Soup over mixture. Bake 1 hour @ 350°.

SERVING SUGGESTIONS:

This is quick and easy. Is good to serve at potlucks.

Margaret Collier
The Great Mosquito Chase
Augusta, Arkansas

Rice Casserole

INGREDIENTS:

1 cup rice (not instant)
1 can onion soup
1 can bouillon soup
1 can drained mushrooms
1/2 stick butter

DIRECTIONS:

Mix all ingredients in casserole, cover and bake at 350° for 1 hour. Stir frequently.

Dana Stetson
Gulf Wind Track Club
Tallahassee, Florida

Classic Corn Casserole

INGREDIENTS:

1 pkg. Jiffy Corn Bread mix
1 stick corn margarine (melted)
2 lrg. eggs
1/2 pt. sour cream
1-15 oz. can cream corn
1-15 oz. can yellow corn (drained)

DIRECTIONS:

Mix all ingredients well in a medium bowl. Pour into a 9" casserole pan and bake in a pre-heated oven at 350° for 1 hour.

Serves 8-10

SERVING SUGGESTIONS:

Morganfield, Kentucky is the county seat of Union County, the top corn producing county in Kentucky. Morganfield is the home of the Corn Festival, which will celebrate its 25th year in 1998. The Corn Classic 5000 Run and Walk has become an important addition to this outstanding tradition. The Classic Corn Casserole recipe was given to Cindy Johnson (wife of the Race Director-Douglas Johnson) from Mrs. Ben Morgan who has served it to her family for many years. It's a favorite at our home and we hope you like it, too.

Douglas J. Johnson, MD
Corn Classic 5000
Morganfield, Kentucky

Sprinter's Sweet Spuds

INGREDIENTS:

3-4 med. size sweet potatoes
1 tblsp. extra virgin olive oil
2 tblsp. pineapple juice
1 tblsp. crushed pineapple
1/2 tsp. cinnamon
1/4 tsp. nutmeg
1/4 tsp. pumpkin pie spice

DIRECTIONS:

Cook potatoes in 300° oven for 1/2 hour. Cut potatoes into strips or pieces like french fries. Brown in olive oil. Add pineapple juice (crushed pineapple if desired). Sprinkle on spices and continue to stir frequently. Do not over cook. May be browned and crisp if desired.

Serves 4-6

SERVING SUGGESTIONS:

Great with poultry of all types.

Zack Subin
Boomer Esiason Foundation, NYC
Boardwalk Runners
Atlantic City, New Jersey

Mexican Rice Casserole

INGREDIENTS:

1 box of Uncle Ben's Rice
1-6 oz. pkg. Long grain & wild rice (original recipe)
1-15 oz. can of black beans
1 cup of frozen corn
1/2 cup picante sauce
1/2 cup grated cheese

DIRECTIONS:

Prepare rice per instructions on the box. Pour rice into bowl, add black beans, corn & picante sauce. Microwave on high for 5-8 minutes. Add grated cheese and let it melt. Serve & enjoy!

Jerry L. Smith
Houston Area Road Runners Association
Sugar Lowe, Texas

Gramma Sylvie's Famous Corn Casserole

INGREDIENTS:

1 cup Velveeta
1 cup butter
1 can cream style corn
2 cups uncooked macaroni

DIRECTIONS:

Melt butter in casserole dish. Cut Velveeta in chunks and add to the melted butter. Add corn (don't drain the whole kernel). Last, add macaroni and stir. Bake uncovered at 350° for 1 hour.

SERVING SUGGESTIONS:

Great for pitch-ins or pot luck meals.

Elaine Doll-Dunn
Black Hills Runners Club
Spearfish, South Dakota

Turkey Trot Squash Casserole

INGREDIENTS:

2 cups cooked & mashed yellow squash
3 carrots (shredded & cooked w/squash)
1 med. onion (chopped & cooked w/squash mixture)
1 can Cream of Chicken Soup
8 oz. sour cream
1 sm. jar pimentos
1 stick butter
8 oz. herb bread stuffing mix

DIRECTIONS:

Cook squash, carrots & onions in water until soft and done, drain. Mix together the soup, sour cream & pimentos. Combine vegetables & soup mixture in a 9"x12" casserole dish. Melt butter & mix the the bread stuffing. Make a layer on the bottom & take out enough to also cover the top. Pour the vegetable mixture over stuffing & remaining stuffing. Let sit in refrigerator for at least a day. Bake 30-40 minutes, covered @ 375°. Uncover and bake 10 more minutes to brown top.

Skip Rogers
Times Turkey Trot
West Florida "Y" Runners Club
Clearwater, Florida

Cheese and Carrot Casserole

INGREDIENTS:

12 med. sliced carrots
1 sm. chopped onion
1/4 cup all purpose flour
2 cups milk
1-8 oz. pkg. American Cheese Slices
1/4 tsp. dry mustard
1/4 tsp. celery salt
dash pepper
dry breadcrumbs

DIRECTIONS:

Preheat oven to 350°. In medium saucepan over medium heat, in 1" boiling water, heat carrots to boiling; cover and cook 20 minutes or until tender-crisp. Drain. Meanwhile, wrap unchopped onion in microwave-safe plastic wrap. Steam on high 2 minutes or until tender. Combine flour and milk in shaker container, transfer to another saucepan. Add onion, salt, dry mustard, celery salt & pepper. Cook mixture, stirring constantly until thickened. Lightly grease 2 quart casserole dish. Spread 1/2 carrots evenly, then half of the cheese. Repeat. Pour sauce over all. Sprinkle with breadcrumbs. Bake uncovered 20 minutes or until hot & bubbly.

Linda Clay
Van Wert Road Runners
Convoy, Ohio

Sandwiches & Pizza

Sandwiches & Pizza

Perfect Pre-Race Pizza

Post-Run Pizza Pie

Spicy Garlic Chicken Pizza

Stuffed Spinach Pizza

Spinach Pizza

Sloppy Julia's

Dad's Philly Steak Sandwiches

Pete's Bodacious Sloppy Joes

Italian Beef Sandwiches

Wenmat Wrap

Perfect Pre-Race Pizza

INGREDIENTS:

cornmeal
frozen pizza crust-thawed
16 oz. tomato sauce
1/4 tsp. basil
1/4 tsp. oregano
dash of salt & pepper
fresh garlic
2-8 oz. pkg. fat free or low fat mozzarella cheese
fat free parmesan cheese

*Optional Toppings - tomato, green, red or yellow peppers, mushrooms, onion, turkey sausage, plain or barbequed chicken

DIRECTIONS:

Preheat oven to 425°. Sprinkle cornmeal on pizza stone. Roll out pizza crust. Using a garlic press spread fresh garlic on crust. In a bowl combine tomato sauce, basil, oregano, salt and pepper mix. Pour over crust. Sprinkle with parmesan cheese. Cover with mozzarella cheese. Add toppings. Place into preheated oven for 10-15 minutes.

SERVING SUGGESTIONS:

Eat as many slices as you wish.

Lauren B. Finnegan
Roadraves Children's Group
Albany, New York

Post-Run Pizza Pie

I N G R E D I E N T S :

pre-made pizza crust
sun-dried tomato/pesto sauce (optional)
olive oil
2 leeks
2 cloves garlic
1 tomato
1/2 brick of feta cheese
greek olives
artichoke hearts
mushrooms

D I R E C T I O N S :

Pre-heat oven to 425°. Dice leeks, garlic and sauté in 1 teaspoon of olive oil on medium heat until very tender (12-15 minutes). Cut tomato, remove seeds and liquid then dice. De-pit olives and dice. Also dice artichoke hearts and mushrooms. Spread olive oil or tomato/pesto sauce on pizza crust. Sprinkle leeks, garlic, tomato, olives, artichoke hearts, mushrooms on crust, then top with grated feta cheese. Bake for 9-11 minutes on oven rack. Remove and let cool for 5 minutes. Cut and serve.

Carla Jackson, Kirk Reynolds
Pomona-Pitzer Colleges Track and Cross Country
Claremont, California

Spicy Garlic Chicken Pizza

INGREDIENTS:

12 oz. boneless chicken breast
1/2 cup sliced green onion
2 cloves minced garlic
2 tblsp. vinegar
2 tblsp. low sodium soy sauce
2 tblsp. olive oil
1/2 tsp. crushed red pepper
1/4 tsp. black pepper
1 tblsp. cornstarch
1 Boboli pizza shell
1/2 cup shredded Monterey Jack Cheese
1/2 cup shredded Mozzarella Cheese
2 tblsp. sliced almonds

DIRECTIONS:

Rinse chicken; pat dry with paper towel. Cut chicken into 1/2" pieces. In large bowl combine half green onion, garlic, vinegar, soy sauce, 1 tablespoon oil, red and black pepper. Add chicken, stir to coat. Let stand 30 minutes @ room temperature. Drain, reserve marinade. Heat remaining oil in large skillet, add chicken. Cook and stir for 3 minutes or until no longer pink. Stir cornstarch into reserved marinade. Add to skillet. Cook and stir until thick and bubbly. Spoon evenly over bread. Sprinkle with cheese. Bake uncovered @ 375° for approximately 12 minutes. Top with remaining green onions, nuts then return to oven for approximately 2 more minutes.

Serves 6

Dean Matanin, Jeneane & Rick
Palmer Good Health Games
Delmont, Pennsylvania

Stuffed Spinach Pizza

INGREDIENTS:

Crust:
1 pkg. dry yeast
1 cup warm water
1 tsp. sugar
1/2 tsp. salt
3 1/2 cup flour
2 tblsp. oil
cornmeal
Filling:
2 cup shredded skim mozzarella
2-5.5 oz. pkg. spinach augratin
1 med. chopped onion
Topping:
8 oz. pizza sauce
1/4 cup fat free parmesan

DIRECTIONS:

Preheat oven to 400°. Dissolve yeast and sugar in warm water. Let stand 5 minutes. Mix flour & salt in large bowl and make a well in center. Work in 1/2 of yeast mixture. Add oil and rest of yeast. Knead for 10 minutes until smooth, then shape into ball. Place in a greased bowl turning dough to grease top. Cover with a damp cloth and let rise in a warm place until doubled 45-60 minutes. Pinch off 2/3 dough. Pat into bottom or sides of 9" deep dish pie plate sprinkled with cornmeal. Layer 1 cup mozzarella, spinach, onion then the rest of mozzarella. Roll out remaining dough to a 13" circle. Place on top of pizza. Pinch together top and bottom crusts. Bake 40 minutes and then spread on pizza sauce & parmesan. Bake 10 minutes more. Let stand 5 minutes before serving.

Carol Seibel & Margaret A. Starnes
RASAC
Streot, Maryland

Spinach Pizza

INGREDIENTS:

1 frozen bread dough or other pizza crust
1 bag fresh spinach
1/8 cup olive oil
1/2 cup parmesan cheese(grated)
crushed garlic
low fat grated mozzarella cheese

DIRECTIONS:

Thaw bread dough (keep covered so it doesn't dry out). Break spinach, discard stems and wash thoroughly. Spin dry and moisten with olive oil. Add parmesan cheese and crushed garlic. Mix. Use garlic to taste. More is better. You may also want to use some garlic powder. Grease pizza pan and add crust, placing mozzarella cheese and spinach on crust. Bake @ 375° for 15-20 minutes or until crust is brown. ENJOY!!

SERVING SUGGESTIONS:

Serve with cold beer for a wonderfully nutritious & healthy meal or party snack (the beer is also good while making the pizza).

John F. Nolan
Wine Glass Running Club
Wellsburg, New York

Sloppy Julias (Joe)

INGREDIENTS:

2 lbs. 90% lean ground beef
1/2 cup onions
1 tblsp. pickle relish
1 cup ketchup
1/2 cup water
2 tblsp. sugar
2 tblsp. mustard
2 tsp. Worcestershire sauce
2 tblsp. vinegar

DIRECTIONS:

Brown ground beef & onions. Add rest of ingredients in a bowl and stir. Add the ingredients from the bowl to the hamburger and simmer for 10 minutes.

SERVING SUGGESTIONS:

In a hurry, it reheats well.

Julia Von Ah
MVRA
Dubuque, Iowa

Dad's Philly Steak Sandwiches

INGREDIENTS:

1/4 lb. thinly sliced steak
1 slice provolone cheese
approx. 2 tblsp. sliced white onion
2 tblsp. sliced green pepper
1 sliced hoagie bun
1 tsp. peanut oil

DIRECTIONS:

Heat 1 tsp. of peanut oil on a non-stick griddle. Sauté the onion and pepper in the oil until heated thoroughly. Add the sliced steak and sauté together until the steak is nearly cooked. Heap the steak and vegetables in the shape of the bun and lay the cheese on top. Open the bun and lay it over the simmering ingredients for 30 seconds. Scoop the ingredients into the bun, and it's ready to serve.

*Note: add salt and pepper to taste when cooking.

Dave Carlson
River Run Road Race
Yankton, South Dakota

Pete's Bodacious Sloppy Joes

INGREDIENTS:

1 sm. peeled and quartered onion
1/4 green pepper, cleaned out and quartered
1 lrg. head of garlic, skins removed and separated into cloves
2 tblsp. butter or margarine
1 1/2 lb. lean hamburger or ground turkey
1-6 oz. can tomato paste
1 1/4 cups water
1 1/2 tsp. garlic salt
1 tsp. chili powder
1/2 tsp. pepper
8 sliced mushrooms
3 or 4 hamburger buns

DIRECTIONS:

Preheat oven to 150°. Place onion, green pepper and garlic in food processor and finely chop. Melt butter in a large skillet at medium heat. Add onion, green pepper, garlic and hamburger. Using a wooden spoon cut hamburger into small pieces and brown lightly, stirring frequently. Add remaining ingredients, reduce heat and simmer 10 minutes, stirring occasionally. Meanwhile, butter both halves of each hamburger bun and warm for 5 minutes in oven. Spoon sloppy joe mix over hamburger buns.

Serves 3-4, (depending on how thick you like them)

SERVING SUGGESTIONS:

A green salad goes well with this wonderfully garlicky dish. So do breath mints if you have company.

Pete Dawson
South Coast Running Club
Coos Bay, Oregon

Italian Beef Sandwiches

INGREDIENTS:

2 pkgs. dry Zesty Italian Dressing
1 pkg. Aujus Mix
2 cups water
2-3 lb. roast
8 lrg. sourdough rolls
8 slices swiss cheese

DIRECTIONS:

Put all ingredients in a crock pot. Cook overnight. Next morning shread roast (most of it falls apart) and cook all day. Serve on sourdough rolls/buns with a slice of cheese.

SERVING SUGGESTIONS:

Make double batch if you are going to have members of your running club over. Easy, easy, recipe!

Julie Ford
Running for the Green
Bentonville, Arkansas

Wenmat Wrap

INGREDIENTS:

2 cups garbanzo beans
1/4 cup fat free plain yogurt
1/4 cup chopped green pepper
1/4 cup diced carrots
lite soy sauce
garlic powder
tortilla or pita

*In this recipe you can use any bean, vegetable or spice you desire.

DIRECTIONS:

Use one 15 oz. can of beans, drain and rinse. Mash with fork or use a Cuisinart. Add pepper and carrots to beans. Add light soy sauce and garlic powder to yogurt according to your own taste. Stir well and then add bean mixture. Coat well. Taste and determine if you would like more soy sauce or garlic. Place approximately 1/2 cup mixture in tortilla and wrap, or place 1/2 mixture in pita bread.

SERVING SUGGESTIONS:

Makes a great lunch sandwich.

Michele Canny Gilles, MPA, RD
Wenmat Sports & Fitness
Carmichael, California

Bread
Basket

Bread Basket

Mr. D's Beer Bread

Carbo-Loading Cinnamon Swirl Quick Bread

Never Fail French Bread

Poppy Seed Bread

Apple Bread

Applesauce Granola Bread

Steve's Cheese and Veggie Adventure Bread

Orange Poppy Seed Bread

Bridget's Irish Soda Bread

Loling's Zucchini Bread

Pumpkin Can Bread

Monkey Bread

Cinnamon Bread

Banana Nut Bread

Honey Banana Nut Bread

Mr. D's Beer Bread

INGREDIENTS:

3 cups self rising flour
1 can of beer of your choice (I like to use Coors, or Corona...very delicate flavor)

DIRECTIONS:

Take a big bowl, six pack of coors & 3 cups of self-rising flour. Mix 1 cup of flour with 1/3 of beer. Mush together. Drink one beer. Place slightly sticky batter in bread pan coated with butter. Drink second beer. Take second cup of flour, put in a bowl add 1/3 beer and moosh it up. Put in bread pan with first third. Ditto on final cup of flour and beer. Put bread pan in oven preheated to 350°. Bake 30-40 minutes, inhaling delicious aromas of hops and cooking bread. Drink another beer.
*Test to make sure it's done, serve with butter, apple butter, etc. and another bottle of beer. After you've put one beer in the recipe and drank the other 5, you don't give a happy rip what it tastes like....but it tastes great!

SERVING SUGGESTIONS:

This bread is hell to slice so you might want to let everyone just break off a chunk. You can also change the taste of the bread by adding stuff like pecans, raisins, etc. prior to cooking.

O. Dewayne Davis
Richmond Times Dispatch Marathon
Richmond, Virginia

"Carbo-Loading" Cinnamon Swirl Quick Bread

INGREDIENTS:

3 cups (divided) sugar
2 tsp. ground cinnamon
4 cups all purpose flour
2 tsp. baking soda
2 cups soured skim milk*
2 egg substitutes
1/2 cup apple butter

Glaze:
3/4 cup confectioners sugar
1/4 tsp. vanilla extract
3-4 tsp. skim milk

DIRECTIONS:

Combine 1 cup sugar and cinnamon; set aside. Combine flour, baking soda and remaining sugar. Combine sour milk, egg substitutes and apple butter. Stir milk mixture into dry ingredients just until combined. Grease the bottoms only of two 9"x5" loaf pans. Pour half of the batter into the bottoms of the 2 pans equally. Sprinkle each pan equally using half of the cinnamon sugar mixed in the recipe. Carefully spread each pan with the remaining batter and sprinkle each with the remaining cinnamon-sugar. Swirl a knife through the batter. Bake at 350° for 45-50 minutes (until a toothpick passes the clean test). Cool in pan 10 minutes before moving to a wire rack to cool completely. Combine glaze ingredients and drizzle over bread.

SERVING SUGGESTIONS:

* To sour milk - mix 1 tsp. lemon juice per 1 cup milk and let stand for 5 minutes before using.

Colleen H. Dye
Utica Roadrunners
Richfield Springs, New York

Never Fail French Bread

INGREDIENTS:

1/4 cup sugar
1/8 cup shortening
2 tsp. salt
1 pint boiling water
2 pkgs. dry yeast
1/2 cup warm water
1 tsp. sugar
6 1/4 cups flour

DIRECTIONS:

Mix first 4 ingredients and allow to cool to lukewarm. Dissolve yeast & sugar in warm water and add to the first mixture, Mix in flour. Work down with a spoon every 10 minutes for an hour. Then divide the dough into 2 parts and roll each part until it is 1/2 inch thick and roll up like a jelly roll. Place on cookie sheet and slash top 2 or 3 times. Let rise until double in bulk. Bake at 400° for 25 minutes or until brown.

SERVING SUGGESTIONS:

To serve slice down to bottom crust and butter. Sprinkle with garlic salt or parmesan cheese. Wrap and heat in oven.

Deborah Warne
Mankato Running Club
Mankato, Kansas

Poppy Seed Bread

INGREDIENTS:

3 cups flour
1 1/2 cups milk
1 1/2 tsp. vanilla
1 1/2 tsp. salt
1 1/2 cups oil
1 1/2 tsp. butter flavoring
1 1/2 tsp. baking powder
2 1/2 cups sugar
1 1/2 tsp almond flavoring
3 eggs
1 1/2 tsp. poppy seeds
Frosting:
Heat together:
1/4 cup orange juice
1 1/2 tsp. vanilla
3/4 cup sugar
1 1/2 tsp. butter flavoring

DIRECTIONS:

Mix all ingredients together and stir until well blended. Pour into 3 aluminum pans. Bake in a 350° oven for over 1 hour. Cool in pan for 5 minutes. Pour frosting over baked bread in pans. Cool 5 minutes in pans. Remove from pans.

Carol Gilbert
Quakerdale Cedar Valley Race
Iowa Falls, Iowa

Apple Bread

INGREDIENTS:

4 cups shredded apples
1 1/2 cups sugar
1/4 cup oil
1/4 cup fat free yogurt
2 eggs well beaten (or substitute Egg Beaters)
2 tblsp. vanilla
2 cups flour
2 tsp. baking soda
2 tsp. cinnamon
1/2 tsp. salt
1 cup chopped nuts

DIRECTIONS:

Grease & flour pans. Mix apples, sugar, oil, eggs, vanilla together. Sift flour, soda, cinnamon & salt together. Add apples to mixture. Mix well. Add nuts. Pour into 2 - 9"x5"x2" loaf pans. Bake @ 350° for 35-45 minutes.

Cathy Howell
SOAR Running Club
Scranton, Pennsylvania

Applesauce Granola Bread

INGREDIENTS:

1 3/4 cup all-purpose flour, use half white and half wheat if desired
2 tsp. baking powder
1/2 tsp. baking soda
1/2 tsp. salt
1 tsp. cinnamon
1/2 tsp. nutmeg
2/3 cup brown sugar
2 1/2 tsp. vegetable oil
1/3 cup nonfat dry milk
1 cup low fat granola
1/2 cup egg substitute or 2 eggs
1 cup + 2 1/2 tblsp. applesauce

DIRECTIONS:

Mix flour, baking powder, salt & baking soda in bowl. In another bowl mix together sugar, cinnamon, nutmeg, oil, nonfat dry milk, granola, egg substitute, and applesauce. Add this mixture to the first bowl. Stir until flour is just moistened. Pour into two non-stick or greased 8"x4" loaf pans or use muffin tins. For loaf pans, bake @ 350° for 40-45 minutes or until they test done. For muffins bake 10-15 minutes. Cool in pans 10 minutes. Remove from pans and finish cooling on a rack. Enjoy this bread at any meal or a snack. *Note-for banana granola bread just substitute mashed banana for applesauce.

Judy Tillapaugh, R.D.
Fort Wayne Track Club
Fort Wayne, Indiana

Steve's Cheese and Veggie Adventure Bread

INGREDIENTS:

*Electric bread machine
1 1/4 cups water
3 tblsp. wheat germ
2 1/2 cups wheat bread flour
1 tblsp. dry milk
1 tsp. salt
2 tblsp. honey
3 tblsp. olive oil
1 cup broccoli & carrots
1 1/2 cup cheddar cheese
1/2 cup sunflower seeds
2 tsp. fast rise yeast

DIRECTIONS:

The easiest way to prepare all these fun ingredients so that they are palatable is to put them in an electric bread maker and push down the button marked start. Should be ready to eat in 4 hours and 10 minutes.

SERVING SUGGESTIONS:

Tastes great warm and served with your very favorite brand of beer (cold) after that long run.

Steve Bainbridge
Running Club North
Fairbanks, Alaska

Orange Poppy Seed Bread

INGREDIENTS:

2 cups all purpose baking flour
2 tsp. baking powder
1/2 tsp. salt
1/3 cup poppy seeds
1/2 cup (4oz.) butter, at room temp.
1 cup sugar
2 lrg. eggs
1 cup milk
1 tsp. vanilla extract
1/2 tsp. orange extract
1/2 tsp. almond extract
grated zest of 1 med. orange (Don't skip this. It makes the bread)

DIRECTIONS:

Preheat oven to 350°. Coat 9"x5"x3" loaf pan with vegetable spray. Mix together dry ingredients. Cream butter and sugar for 3 minutes or until light and fluffy. Beat in eggs, one at a time. Add milk, extract and zest. On low speed, blend in dry ingredients until combined. Do not over mix! Spoon batter into pan, smoothing on top. Bake 1 hour, 15 minutes or until tester comes out clean. Allow to cool for 10 minutes before removing from the pan.

SERVING SUGGESTIONS:

Cool completely to make slicing easier.

Nancy Caviness
"Advice 5K" Annual Turkey Trot
Duck, North Carolina

Bridget's Irish Soda Bread

INGREDIENTS:

3 1/2 cup flour
1 tsp. soda
1 tsp. baking powder
2/3 cup sugar
1 tsp. salt
2 beaten eggs
1 1/2 cup buttermilk
2 tsp. melted butter
1 1/2 cup raisins
1 tsp. orange rind

DIRECTIONS:

Sift together dry ingredients. Add raisins. Mix in other ingredients. Pour in greased loaf pan. Bake for 1 hour @ 375°.

Eileen R. Hagan
Annapolis Striders
Annapolis, Maryland

Loling's Zucchini Bread

INGREDIENTS:

2 cups flour
2 tsp. baking soda
1 tsp. salt
1/4 tsp. baking powder
3 tsp. cinnamon
3 eggs
1 cup vegetable oil
1 1/2 cups of sugar or 1 cup honey
2 cups of zucchini grated (2 med. sized)
2 tsp. vanilla
1 cup raisins
1 cup chopped walnuts
1/2 cup chopped cranberries

DIRECTIONS:

Sift together, flour, baking soda, salt, baking powder, cinnamon. Combine eggs, oil, sugar, zucchini, vanilla in large bowl & beat until mixed. Stir in flour mixture until smooth. Stir in raisins, nuts and berries. Pour into greased 13"x9"x2" loaf pan or 4 small loaf pans. Bake @ 350° or until done, approximately 30 minutes for small pans. Cool on wire rack.

SERVING SUGGESTIONS:

Makes a great snack on the go. Freeze extra loaves for later. Top with cream cheese or powdered sugar on slice of bread for extra flavor.

Kellie McGrath
Alton Parks and Recreation
Alton, New Hampshire

Pumpkin Can Bread

INGREDIENTS:

1 cup oil
1 cup pumpkin
2 1/2 cups sugar
4 eggs
2/3 cups water
1 tsp. nutmeg
1 tsp. cinnamon
1 tsp. salt
2 tblsp. baking soda
3 cups flour
1 cup raisins

DIRECTIONS:

Grease and flour 3 coffee cans. Mix all ingredients and pour into the 3 cans.
Bake at 350° for 1 hour. Each can will be approximately half full.

Nancy & Pete Wilderotter
Central Jersey Road Runners Club
New Providence, New Jersey

Monkey Bread

INGREDIENTS:

2 cans jumbo biscuits
1 1/2 tsp. cinnamon
3/4 cup granular sugar
3/4 stick margarine(melted)
nuts (optional)
meats (optional)
raisins (optional)
Sugar frosting:
2 1/2 cups confectioners sugar
1/2 tsp. vanilla extract
few drops of water

DIRECTIONS:

Mix cinnamon & sugar in a bowl. Grease pan (angel food cake tin works great and looks good when finished with melted butter). Place nuts, meats, raisins or whatever is desirable in the bottom of the pan. Cut each biscuit into quarters and toss into sugar and cinnamon mixture, place in large bowl. Any sugar ingredients that are left, pour over the cut biscuits, toss to cover all. Place evenly in bottom of tube pan.

Pour remainder of melted margarine over biscuits. Let set while oven pre-heats to 350°. Bake for 30-35 minutes. Remove and let cool for 5 minutes. Cut around tube pan and invert onto large plate. When cool pour frosting over bread. *When mixing frosting, make sure it is not to thin or bread is not too warm. Pour over bread (if it is too hot the bread will absorb all the frosting).

SERVING SUGGESTIONS:

This can be served as a bread or like a dessert. Slice and place on a plate to be torn apart like finger food. This is best served after a long run out the back of a pick-up truck in the woods with your friends. Gatorade goes good with bread.

John Holmes
Croom Trail Runners of Florida
Pinellas Park, Florida

Cheese Bread

INGREDIENTS:

1 med. egg
1 tsp. dehydrated onion flakes
1 oz. lowfat sharp cheddar cheese(diced)
1/2 cup skim milk
1 crumbled slice lite bread

DIRECTIONS:

Mix all ingredients and bake in an 8 oz. baking dish at 350° until golden brown (for about 15 minutes).

Melanie R. Rudolph
Muncie, Indiana

Ken's Broccoli Bread

INGREDIENTS:

1 pkg. frozen chopped broccoli
1 pkg. Jiffy Corn Bread Mix
6 oz. cottage cheese
1 stick lowfat melted margarine
1/4 cup minced onion
4 eggs (can use Egg Beaters)
1/2 cup cheddar cheese

DIRECTIONS:

Cook broccoli. Mix remaining ingredients well. Drain and stir in broccoli.
Put in 9"x13" pan or iron skillet. Bake @ 350° for 30 minutes.

SERVING SUGGESTIONS:

Great with any kind of soup.

> *Ken Jessee*
> Huntsville Track Club
> Huntsville, Alabama

Cinnamon Bread

I N G R E D I E N T S :

Batter:
1/2 cup shortening
2 cups sugar
2 eggs
2 cups buttermilk (buy qt. and freeze other half)
2 tsp. baking soda
4 cups flour
1 tsp. salt
Topping:
3/4 cup sugar
2 tblsp. cinnamon

D I R E C T I O N S :

Mix ingredients in order given until batter is smooth. Pour batter into the bottom of 2 greased loaf pans to the depth of about 1 inch. Sprinkle 1/2 topping over batter. Then pour remaining batter over that layer and then the remaining topping over that. Use a knife to swirl topping through batter. Bake @ 350° for 55 minutes.

Makes 2 loaves

S E R V I N G   S U G G E S T I O N S :

This is a very easy to make recipe. The bread freezes well so you can make it and use it whenever you need it. It's a great for school snacks, after school snacks, lunches, or late night snacks. Just slice and eat or you may wish to spread some butter or margarine on it.

Nancy & Brant Tolsma
Liberty University Track & Field
Liberty, Virginia

Banana Nut Bread

I N G R E D I E N T S :

1 3/4 cup flour
2 tsp. baking powder
1/2 tsp. salt
1/4 tsp. baking soda
2/3 cup sugar
2/3 cup applesauce
3 mashed bananas
1 cup chopped walnuts

D I R E C T I O N S :

Combine all dry ingredients. Add applesauce & bananas. Stir in walnuts.
Pour into greased & floured loaf pan (9"x5"x3"). Bake @ 350° for 45-60
minutes.

Derek Ammons
Annapolis Striders
Laurell, Maryland

Honey Banana Nut Bread

INGREDIENTS:

1 cup butter
1 cup honey
2 eggs, beaten
1 cup chopped nuts
3 bananas
2 cups sifted flour
1 tsp. baking soda
1/2 tsp. vanilla

DIRECTIONS:

Cream butter and honey. Add beaten eggs. Cream bananas until fluffy. Add to the sugar mixture alternately with the dry ingredients. Add chopped nuts. Pour mixture into a greased loaf pan and bake @ 350° for 1 hour.

Dr. Keith Cooper
Port City Pacers, Mobile Alabama
Pensacola Runners Association, Florida

Notes

Sweet Finishes

Sweet Finishes

Race Director Carrot Cake
Portland Marathon Can't Resit'em Cookies
10 K Cookies
The Elegant Luscious Cheesecake
Carrot Deluxe Cake
Trail Cookies
Columbus Marathon Meringue Cookies
Rocky Mountain Pie
"Better Than Sex" Cake
Joline's Chocolate Cake
Quick Upside Down Apple Cake
Mrs. D's Easy One Bowl Apple Cake
Low Fat Chocolate Wacky Cake
Aunt Debbies French Apple Pie
Yogurt Pudding
Colorado Carmelleta's
Double Chocolate Biscotti
Cassava Cake
Mikes Energy Cookies
Pumpkin Cookies
Peanut Butter Carob Brownies
J.T.'s Power Cookies
Jim's Sweet Potato Pie
Go-Go Bars
Grandma Debby's Fuit Pie
Lemon Bars
Helen's Candy Bar Pie
Peanut Butter M&M Cookies
Cherry Torte
Cathy's Cheesecake
Banana Oatmeal Cookies
Good For You Pumpkin Pie
Low Fat Peach Bundt Cake
Mamie's Pound Cake
"Guilt Free" Brownies
Buckeye Candy

Race Director Carrot Cake

INGREDIENTS:

6 1/4 cups corn oil
10 cups sugar
10 cups flour
4 tblsp. cinnamon
3 tblsp. + 1 tsp. baking powder
1 tblsp. + 2 tsp. baking soda
1 tblsp. + 2 tsp. salt
24 eggs
20 cups grated carrots

5 cups chopped walnuts
5 cups raisins
Cream cheese frosting:
32 oz. softened butter
32 oz. softened cream cheese
4-1 lb. boxes of powdered sugar
4 tsp. vanilla extract

DIRECTIONS:

Preheat oven (large) to 350°. Spray 18"x24" pan with Pam & flour. Beat together oil and sugar, whisk in eggs. Sift together dry ingredients and slowly add to sugar/oil/eggs combo. When mixed add carrots, then walnuts, & raisin. This all takes a bit of muscle. How long to bake? Good question. Until center springs back when lightly touched. At least 70 minutes but keep checking to make sure not to over cook. Can be made a couple days in advance, which is important since packet pickup is always difficult the day before the race. Once cool, flip it over onto a very large cookie sheet, wrap in plastic wrap until time to frost.

Frosting: Beat cream cheese & butter together, add sugar, & vanilla. Frost shortly before bringing to race.

SERVING SUGGESTIONS:

*Three of these cakes do nicely for 400 racers. Bring a large knife to race. Make sure that a volunteer precuts cake to facilitate going through the food line.

Maureen Giuffre, R.N., Ph.D.
Mid-Delmarva Family YMCA
Salisbury, Maryland

Portland Marathon Can't Resist 'Em Cookies

INGREDIENTS:

good

1 cup (2 sticks) butter or margarine
1 cup firmly packed brown sugar
1/4 cup granulated sugar
2 eggs
1 tsp. vanilla
1 cup wheat flour
1/2 cup white flour
1 tsp. baking soda
3 cups oatmeal (of high quality with large oat flakes)
1/4 cup chocolate chips
1/4 cup golden raisins
1/4 cup toasted coconut flakes
1/2 cup walnuts

DIRECTIONS:

First toast coconut flakes by pouring them on a cookie sheet & placing them in the oven at 200° for 20-30 minutes or until slightly golden brown. Cream butter & sugars. Add eggs & vanilla. Slowly stir in both flours & baking soda. Mix in the oatmeal. Finally, add chocolate chips, raisins, coconut & walnuts. Heat oven to 350°. Lightly spray the cookie sheet with Pam (or other non-stick spray). Place rounded tablespoons of stiff batter on cookie sheet. Bake 8-10 minutes or until golden brown.

SERVING SUGGESTIONS:

Eat after a hard run or when you're in the mood for a tasty, wholesome snack!

Les Smith
Portland Marathon
Portland, Oregon

10 K Cookies

INGREDIENTS:

1 egg or egg substitute
2 sticks, sweet unsalted "I Can't Believe It's Not Butter"
1/2 cup dark brown sugar
1/2 cup white sugar
1 tsp. baking soda
1 tsp. pumpkin pie spice
1/2 cup applesauce (or pumpkin)
1 3/4 unbleached all purpose flour
1-1 1/2 cups oatmeal
12 oz. chocolate chips (or split w/1/2 peanut butter chips, or 1/2 raisins) (in the summer use fresh blueberries)

DIRECTIONS:

Soften butter, mix in sugars, beat in egg, baking soda & spice. Stir in applesauce (or pumpkin). Fold in partial amounts of flour. Stir in oatmeal. Fold in chips, raisins, or blueberries. Drop onto cookie sheets. Bake in pre-heated 350° oven for 12-15 minutes.

SERVING SUGGESTIONS:

Use less sugar...more moist (with applesauce)...healthier (with oatmeal).

Suzanne M. Elward
North Jersey Masters
Whippany, New Jersey

The Elegant Luscious Cheesecake

INGREDIENTS:

32 oz. cream cheese (not Low Fat)
8 oz. heavy cream
8 oz. sour cream
4-5 eggs
1 tblsp. vanilla
1 1/2 cups powdered sugar
Crust:
1/4 cup butter
1/4 cup sugar
1 cup oreo cookie crumbs

DIRECTIONS:

First make crust. Place in bottom of 10" spring pan, but don't pack too tightly. Let ingredients of cake warm to room temperature. Then mix together - don't over beat. If needed, warm very slightly to smooth out lumps. The powdered sugar is the secret to a smooth texture. Bake at 325° for 1 hour, 15 minutes. Then turn oven off & leave in closed oven for a couple hours. Refrigerate 3 hours before serving. If the top cracks, float some fruit on top to cover.

SERVING SUGGESTIONS:

A little Amaretto or Frangelico liqueur drizzled on top just before serving adds a great touch. This cheesecake is so rich, only a small slice is needed for satisfaction.

Bob Wuest
Run Tex - The Runners Store
Austin, Texas

Carrot Cake Deluxe

INGREDIENTS:

3 cups sifted all-purpose flour
2 cups sugar
4 lrg. eggs at room temperature
1 cup whole milk
4 tsp. lemon juice
1 tsp. vanilla
2 tsp. baking soda
2 rounded tsp. cinnamon
1 1/2 cups Canola oil

1 1/2 cups chopped walnuts
5-6 peeled & grated carrots
Frosting:
3+ cups confectionary sugar
6 oz. softened cream cheese
1/3 cup Crisco
3 tsp. light rum
zest from orange, finely chopped
1 tblsp. milk

DIRECTIONS:

Beat sugar, eggs, vanilla, 3 tsp. lemon juice at medium speed. Combine flour, baking soda, salt, & cinnamon in bowl & blend together with whisk. Add to mixing bowl with eggs, oil & milk (with 1 tsp. lemon juice in milk). Beat at medium speed until well blended. Fold in chopped walnuts & grated carrots with large spoon. Pour into 9-11 cup bundt cake pan after spraying inside with Baker's Joy. Bake at 300° on middle shelf of oven for 1 1/2 hours. Allow to cool on wire rack for 1-2 hours. Beat frosting ingredients together until smooth. Frost cake when cooled.

SERVING SUGGESTIONS:

Cake should be refrigerated before serving and served with coffee or tea. Cake should be covered with film and refrigerated to preserve freshness after cutting.

Chef Frank Lusito
Poughkeepsie, New York

Trail Cookies

INGREDIENTS:

1 box Spice Cake mix (any brand)
1/2 cup water or soy milk
2 eggs
3/4 cup Canola oil
2 cups oatmeal
1 cup raisins
1 cup dried cranberries
1/4 cup brown sugar
1/2 cup nuts (optional)
1 tsp. cinnamon
1 tsp. nutmeg
1 tsp. allspice

DIRECTIONS:

Mix all ingredients. Drop spoonfuls onto slightly greased tray. Bake at 350° for 8-10 minutes. (Best consistency is a bit on the gooey side).

SERVING SUGGESTIONS:

Replenish calories from your trail run!

Nancy Hobbs
All American Trail Running Association
Colorado Springs, Colorado

Columbus Marathon Meringue Cookies

INGREDIENTS:

2 egg whites
pinch of salt
1/2 tsp. cream of tartar
3/4 cup sugar
1/4 tsp. peppermint extract
2-3 drops green food coloring (optional)
6 oz. chocolate chips

DIRECTIONS:

Beat egg whites, salt & cream of tartar until stiff. Add sugar, peppermint extract & food coloring. Fold chocolate chips in lightly. Drop tablespoonfuls of batter onto cookie sheets covered with waxed paper. Preheat oven to 350° for 15 minutes. TURN OVEN OFF. Put cookies into oven. Leave overnight or 5-6 hours until firm.

Makes 3 dozen cookies.

Joan Riegel
Columbus Marathon
Columbus, Ohio

Run for the Kitchen

Rocky Mountain Pie

INGREDIENTS:

1/2 cup butter or margarine
2 eggs
1 cup sugar
1/2 cup flour
1/4 cup bourbon
1 tsp. vanilla
1 cup chopped walnuts or pecans
1 cup chocolate chips
9" unbaked pie shell

DIRECTIONS:

Cream butter & sugar. Add eggs and mix well. Add flour, stir, then mix in remaining ingredients. Pour mixture into unbaked pie shell. Bake at 375° for 40 minutes. Serve warm with whipped cream or vanilla ice cream.

This is the world's best pie! A friend of ours gives me a small bottle of bourbon each Christmas so I don't have an excuse for not making this pie. My husband and I first had this pie at a resort in Pagosa Springs, Colorado. We loved it from the very first piece! We came home and tried to duplicate it-no luck. Even memorized a few recipes while in culinary shops to avoid buying 'another' cookbook-no luck. Finally my sister and her husband were going to be in Pagosa Springs so we asked them to visit this resort and try the RM pie and to let us know what we were missing. After eating the pie, she asked the waitress for the recipe, which they had already copied to make available for their patrons.

Susan Alexander
Mesa Monument Striders
Whitewater, Colorado

"Better Than Sex" Cake

INGREDIENTS:

1 German Chocolate cake mix
1 jar caramel ice cream topping
1 tub Cool Whip
1 can sweetened condensed milk
2 Heath or Skor candy bars

DIRECTIONS:

Follow box directions for cake mix. Remove from oven & cool for 5 minutes. Use wooden spoon handle to poke holes in cake. Pour one can sweetened condensed milk over cake; then pour the caramel topping over the cake. Cool for 1 hour in fridge. Top with Cool Whip & crushed candy bars. Chill until ready to serve. Look out, this is addictive!

Doug Slaton
Galesburg Road Runners Club
Knoxville, Illionis

Joline's Chocolate Cake

INGREDIENTS:

1 cup water
2 eggs
1/2 cup butter
1 1/2 squares chocolate
2 cups flour
2 cups sugar
1/2 cup (6 oz.) sour cream
1 tsp. baking soda
1/2 tblsp. salt
<u>Frosting:</u>
1/2 cup oleo
1 1/2 squares chocolate
4 1/2 cup sifted powdered sugar
1 tsp. vanilla
6 tblsp. (1/3 cup) milk
pecan halves

DIRECTIONS:

Combine water, butter & chocolate in saucepan. Bring to boil & remove
from heat. Mix flour & sugar together. Stir in flour & sugar mixture. Add
eggs, sour cream, soda & salt. Mix well & bake in greased pan at 375°.
*<u>Frosting:</u> Combine butter, milk & chocolate in saucepan. Boil 1 minute.
Remove & add sugar. Beat until smooth. Stir in vanilla. Frost cake & garnish with pecan halves.

SERVING SUGGESTIONS:

Consume 1 slice before a 10K, 2 slices before a half marathon.

Louis Joline
Kansas City Track Club
Lake Lotawana, Missouri

Quick Upside Down Apple Cake

INGREDIENTS:

Topping:
1/4 tsp. cinnamon
3 cups peeled, diced apples
1/4 cup apple sauce
Cake:
2 egg whites
1/4 cup applesauce
1/2 tsp. cinnamon
1/2 cup apple juice
1 tblsp. orange juice concentrate
3 tblsp. unsweetened pineapple juice
1 1/2 cup all-purpose flour
1 1/4 tsp. baking soda

DIRECTIONS:

Preheat oven to 350°. Spray 8"x 8"x 2" pan. To prepare topping, toss together apples, applesauce & cinnamon in a large bowl. Smooth topping into the bottom of the pan. Mix flour, baking soda, pineapple juice, apple juice, orange juice, applesauce, cinnamon & egg whites together. Stir well & pour over the topping in the pan. Bake in preheated oven at 350° for 30 minutes. Reduce oven to 325° & bake for 5 more minutes or until cake tester comes out clean. Remove pan from oven & place on a wire rack. Cool for 20 minutes before loosening the cake. Turn the cake upside down on a platter. Cut into 3"x 3" pieces.

Executive Chef Richard Robinson
Provena Saint Joseph Medical Center Racing Hearts
Joliet, Illinois

Mrs. D's Easy
One Bowl Apple Cake

INGREDIENTS:

2 cups finely diced, peeled apples
1 cup sugar (may be cut in half)
1/4 cup vegetable oil
1 egg
1/2 cup raisins (optional)
1 cup unsifted flour
1 tsp. cinnamon
1 tsp. baking soda
1/4 tsp. salt
1 tsp. vanilla
1/2 cup chopped nuts (optional)

DIRECTIONS:

In a bowl, place diced apples. Add sugar & raisins. Let stand for approximately 15 minutes. Add vegetable oil & egg. Mix together well with spoon. Sift flour, cinnamon, baking soda & salt into apple mixture. Stir to mix. Add vanilla & nuts and stir. Pour into sprayed & floured 8"x8" pan. Bake at 350° for 40-45 minutes or until cake tester comes out clean. Cool in pan for 10 minutes. Turn onto rack. May top with confectionary sugar, ice cream or whipped cream.

SERVING SUGGESTIONS:

I enjoy this recipe, for you can easily 1 1/2 or double the recipe by baking in a 13"x9" baking pan. You can also use part whole wheat flour.

Susan Reh Riley
Long Island Cares' Harry Chapin 5K Run Against Hunger
West Brentwood, New York

Low Fat Chocolate Wacky Cake

INGREDIENTS:

2 1/2 cups flour
2 cups sugar
2 tsp. soda
3/4 cup cocoa
1 tsp. salt
2 tsp. vanilla
2 tblsp. vinegar
5 tblsp. canola oil
5 tblsp. applesauce

DIRECTIONS:

Combine all ingredients with 2 cups cold water in large mixing bowl. Beat for about 2 minutes or until smooth. Pour into 9"x13" greased & floured pan. Bake @ 350° for 40-45 minutes. Test with toothpick. Very moist & so yummy!

SERVING SUGGESTIONS:

I usually don't frost this cake (it's so moist & sweet, I don't think it needs it). The recipe is correct - no eggs, no milk. So easy!

Cindy Hight
Southeast Kansas Grand Prix
Riverton, KS
Baxter Springs Cowtown 5K Run
Baxter Springs, Kansas

Aunt Debbie's French Apple Pie

INGREDIENTS:

1-10" pie crust
2 cups flour
3/4 tsp. salt
1/2 cups & 2 tblsp. shortening
1/3 cup boiling water
1 tsp. vinegar
Filling:
1 cup sugar
8-10 cored, peeled & sliced med. green tart apples
3 tsp. cinnamon
1/2 tsp. nutmeg
1/2 tsp. cloves
2 tblsp. cornstarch
butter
Crumb Topping:
1/3 cup sugar
3/4 cup flour
6 tblsp. butter
1 tsp. cinnamon

DIRECTIONS:

Cut shortening into flour & salt. Add boiling water & vinegar. Form into ball & handle lightly. Mix all ingredients for filling together. Fill pie pastry with apples. Top apples with dabs of butter, 1 chunk every 3".
Crumb Topping: Mix sugar, flour & cinnamon. Cut in butter. Sprinkle over apples. Bake pie at 350°for 50-60 minutes or until apples are soft.

Randy Mitchell
Springville Apple Run
Springville, California

Yogurt Pudding

INGREDIENTS:

16 oz. plain non-fat yogurt
2-3 oz. sugar free non-fat instant pudding (any flavor)

DIRECTIONS:

Mix ingredients. Refrigerate & serve at room temperature.

SERVING SUGGESTIONS:

Sprinkle with chopped nuts, granola, or your favorite topping. Serve.

Joyce Barrett
Boston Athletic Association
Attleboro, Massachusetts

Colorado Carmelleta's

INGREDIENTS:

1 cup flour
1 cup oats
3/4 cup brown sugar
1/2 tsp. baking soda
1/4 tsp. salt
3/4 cup (1 1/2 sticks) melted butter
1 cup dark chocolate chips
3/4 cup caramel topping
3 tblsp. flour

DIRECTIONS:

Combine all first 6 ingredients. Grease 9"x9" baking dish, line bottom of dish using 1/2 of mixture and bake for 10 minutes at 350°. Combine dark chocolate chips, caramel topping & flour. Spread mixture over the "crust" in the baking dish. Spread the second half of the flour & oats mixture over the caramel & chocolate chip layer. Bake on second rack of oven at 350° for 15 minutes or until golden brown.

Pat Downing
The Downing Group
Englewood, Colorado

Double Chocolate Biscotti

INGREDIENTS:

2 cups flour
1/2 cup cocoa powder
1 tsp. baking soda
1 tsp. salt
1 stick butter
1 cup sugar
2 eggs
1 cup chocolate chips
1 tsp. cinnamon
1 tsp. vanilla

DIRECTIONS:

Preheat oven to 350°. Line a baking pan with wax paper/parchment paper. In a bowl, stir together all dry ingredients except sugar, with an electric mixer. In another bowl, beat butter & sugar until light & fluffy. Add eggs one at a time & combine well. Add vanilla. Stir in flour to form a stiff dough. Add chocolate chips last. Form dough into 2 logs (12"x2"). Slightly flatten & sprinkle with powdered sugar. Bake 30 minutes or until firm to the touch. Cool Biscotti & slice Biscotti into 3/4" slices & arrange cut side down on baking sheet. Bake until slightly crisp, 8 minutes. Cool and store in air-tight container.

Liz Kane
Martha's Athletic Club
Edgartown, Massachusetts

Cassava Cake

I N G R E D I E N T S :

4 cups fresh yuca (2 1/2 lbs.)
8 oz. can coconut milk
2 eggs
2 cups sugar
8 oz. bar low fat cream cheese
1/2 cup condensed milk

D I R E C T I O N S :

Preheat oven to 375°. Line a 8"x11" pan with wax paper, than grease. Peel and grate or shred yuca. Save 1 egg yolk for wash. Beat eggs and add sugar. Mix thoroughly. Add yuca & 7/8 of coconut milk. Mix well and place in prepared pan. Bake for 20 minutes. To make egg wash, mix egg yolk & 1/8 coconut milk together. Brush on top of yuca. Bake another 10 minutes, or until done. Put in broiler to brown top. Let cool and cut into wedges. Decorate with fresh fruit on the side.

Marissa S. de Luna
U.S.A.T.F. Metropolitan Athletics Congress
New York, New York

Mike's Energy Cookies

INGREDIENTS:

1 cup sugar
1/2 cup peanut butter
1/3 cup honey
2 cups oats
2 cups flour
1 tsp. vanilla
4 egg whites
1/4 tsp. salt
1 1/2 tsp. cinnamon
1 tsp. baking soda
4 tblsp. water(or maybe more)

DIRECTIONS:

Mix ingredients well; roll into balls (if your hands are wet, the dough doesn't stick as much). Flatten out balls with a fork (dip fork in water between each cookie to prevent sticking). Bake on an insulated cookie sheet (coated liberally with Pam) in a 325° oven for 18 minutes. Cooking time will be less if you use a non-insulated cookie sheet.

SERVING SUGGESTIONS:

The dough is very hard to mix (this counts as an upper extremity workout)! Also, the dough or even the cookies can be frozen if needed.

Michael Boone
Thunder in the Hills 5K
Hillsboro, Ohio

Pumpkin Cookies

INGREDIENTS:

2 eggs
1 1/2 cup sugar
3/4 cup oil
1 1/2 cup canned pumpkin
2 3/4 cup flour
1 1/2 tsp. baking powder
1/2 tsp. salt
1/2 tsp. baking soda
1 1/2 tsp. cinnamon
1 1/2 tsp. vanilla
Icing:
1 cup powdered sugar
2 tsp. milk

DIRECTIONS:

Mix all ingredients together well. Drop from teaspoon onto greased cookie sheet. Bake at 350° for 15 minutes. Ice each cookie with powdered sugar icing.

Ida N. Gorman
Turkey Trek
Mechanicsburg, Pennsylvania

Peanut Butter Carob Brownies

INGREDIENTS:

1 cup all-purpose flour
3/4 tsp. baking powder
1/4 tsp. salt
1 cup packed brown sugar
1 egg (or egg substitute)
5 tsp. melted margarine
1 tsp. vanilla
1 cup carob powder
1/3 cup peanut butter

DIRECTIONS:

Stir flour with baking powder & salt. Cream together sugar, egg, margarine & vanilla. Gradually stir in flour mixture until well blended. Stir in carob powder & peanut butter. Spread evenly into well-greased 8" pan. Bake at 350° for 30 minutes. Cool in pan. Cut into 20 bars.

SERVING SUGGESTIONS:

Top with a scoop of vanilla frozen yogurt, if desired.

Lisa Cook
Bethel Half Marathon
Canton, North Carolina

J.T.'s Power Cookies

INGREDIENTS:

2 cups brown sugar
1/4 cup vegetable oil
1/4 to 1/3 cup applesauce or another mashed fruit
1/2 cup egg substitute or 2 eggs
1 cup non-fat dry milk
2 tsp. almond, rum, vanilla, or coconut extract
1/4 tsp. salt
1 tsp. baking soda
2 1/4 cups flour, if desired use 1/2 whole wheat and 1/2 white flour
2 cups quick oats
1 cup raisins or any chopped dried fruit
1/2 cup chocolate chips (optional)

DIRECTIONS:

In a mixing bowl combine sugar, oil & applesauce until well blended. Stir in egg substitute, non-fat dry milk, flavored extract & salt. Then stir in flour & baking soda. Finally add oats, fruit & chocolate chips. If batter needs more moisture add a little more applesauce. Drop dough by teaspoons, 2" apart onto a non-stick cookie sheet. Bake in a pre-heated 350° oven for 10-15 minutes or until they test done. Remove from cookie sheet & cool.

SERVING SUGGESTIONS:

Serve as a snack or a dessert. Re-fuel after a long run by having a couple cookies! Store unused cookies in an airtight container or freeze them for later use. Enjoy!

Judy Tillapaugh, R.D.
Fort Wayne Track Club
Fort Wayne, Indiana

Jim's Sweet Potato Pie

I N G R E D I E N T S :

1 1/2 lbs. sweet potatoes (approximately 5 potatoes)
3/4 cup white or brown sugar
1 tsp. cinnamon
1/2 tsp. nutmeg
2 pinches ground cloves
1 pinch salt
1/4 tsp. vanilla
2 drops lemon flavoring
3 eggs
1 cup heavy cream
1 pie crust (bottom)

D I R E C T I O N S :

Preheat oven to 425°. Peel slice and boil sweet potatoes. Drain & mash until mostly delumped (if using electric mixer, use a low setting). Mix yams with dry ingredients and lemon extract. In a separate bowl, lightly beat eggs & cream together. Pour egg/cream mixture into yams and blend. Pour mixture into pie crust. Bake at 425° for 15 minutes and then at 325° for 35-40 minutes until center is set.

Carla C. Hickey
Lehigh River Relay Run
Allentown, Pennsylvania

Go-Go Bars

INGREDIENTS:

1 cup Karo syrup
1 cup sugar
1 cup peanut butter
6 cups Rice Crispy Cereal
1/2 cup chocolate chips
1/2 cup butterscotch chips

DIRECTIONS:

In large pot, bring sugar and karo syrup to just a boil. Remove from heat and add peanut butter. Mix well. Add Rice Crispy, mix. Put mixture into a 13"x9" pan, spread evenly. In a small sauce pan melt chocolate and butterscotch chips together slowly until completely smooth. Spread evenly over bars. Let set for about 1 hour. Enjoy!

Lori L. Seog
Penacook Community Center
Penacook, New Hampshire

Grandma Debby's Fruit Pie

INGREDIENTS:

2-9" baked pie shells
1/2 cup flour or 3 tsp. cornstarch.
1 can crushed pineapple
3 oz. pkg. strawberry jello
1-10 oz. pkg. frozen strawberries
4 med. bananas
1 cup pecans
cool whip

DIRECTIONS:

Combine flour or cornstarch and pineapple in a saucepan. Cook until thick. Add jello. Stir until thick. Add jello and stir until dissolved. Add strawberries and let cool. Add 2 sliced bananas and pecans. Line each pie shell with one banana. Pour mixture into shells. Top with cool whip. Refrigerate.

Deborah J. Ritter
Longview Running Club
Marshall, Texas

Lemon Bars

INGREDIENTS:

1 box of 1 step Angel Food cake mix
powdered sugar
lemon extract
1-21 oz. can lemon pie filling

DIRECTIONS:

With a spoon, stir together cake mix and pie filling. Do not use mixer. Pour into ungreased 10 1/2"x15 1/2" pan. Bake at 350° for 20-25 minutes. When cool, frost with a powdered sugar frosting with lemon extract.

Melanie R. Rudolph
Munice, Indiana

Helen's Candy Bar Pie

INGREDIENTS:

4 sm. Hershey Almond candy bars
1/2 cup milk
lrg. marshmallows
1/2 pint cool whip
pie crust

DIRECTIONS:

Break up 4 small Hershey Almond candy bars and combine this with 1/2 cup of milk and 18 large marshmallows. Heat all of this until melted and well blended, stirring constantly. Then chill thoroughly. Whip 1/2 pint whipping cream, then use beater to whip up the thickened candy mixture. Fold cream into candy mixture. Pour into baked pie crust and chill several hours before serving. A little grated chocolate on the top makes it pretty too. *I buy the pack of six hershey's milk chocolate with almonds, put four in the pie, grate another bar on top and Milt, my husband eats the sixth bar.

Helen Brown
Club Kokomo Roadrunners
Kokomo, Indiana

Peanut Butter M&M Cookies

INGREDIENTS:

1 cup peanut butter
1 cup margarine
1 cup brown sugar
1 cup sugar
2 eggs
2 tsp. vanilla
2 1/2 cups flour
1 1/2 tsp. salt
1/2 tsp. soda
1-16 oz. bag plain M&M's

DIRECTIONS:

Preheat oven to 350°. Cream peanut butter, margarine & sugars. Add eggs & vanilla. Add flour, salt & soda, mixing it well. Reserve 1/2 cup of M&M's and stir in remaining. Lightly grease cookie sheets and drop 1/4 cup dough 2 inches apart (they will spread). Gently press in 3 or 4 M&M's on the top of each. Bake 15-20 minutes until golden brown on the edges.

SERVING SUGGESTIONS:

A great treat after that tough workout!!

Susan Waterbury
San Luis Distance Club
San Luis Obispo, Connecticut

Cherry Pie Torte

INGREDIENTS:

1 cup butter
2 cups pretzels, coarsely ground
3/4 cup sugar
1 can cherry pie filling
2-8 oz. cream cheese
1 cup powdered sugar
1-8 oz. cool whip

DIRECTIONS:

Melt butter with sugar & pretzels. Spread into 9"x13" pan, reserving 1/4 for the topping. Blend cream cheese and powdered sugar. Spread over cooled pretzel crust. Cover with pie filling. Then add cool whip and left over pretzel topping.

Mary Doyle Lehman
"Strain for the Brain" Run
West Allis, Wisconsin

Cathy's Cheesecake

INGREDIENTS:

Crust:
2 cups low fat crushed graham crackers
1/4 cup sugar
1/4 cup melted margarine
Filling:
2 lbs. (4-8 oz. pkgs.) non-fat cream cheese, at room temperature
1 1/4 cups sugar
5 eggs
2 1/2 tblsp. lemon juice
1 1/2 pints (3 cups) non-fat sour cream
2 tsp. vanilla or almond flavoring

DIRECTIONS:

Crust: Mix ingredients together well. Press firmly into a 9 or 10 inch spring form pan. Chill.
Filling: On low speed with mixer, blend cream cheese. Add sugar and eggs, continuing at low speed. Blend in lemon juice & flavoring. Gently fold in sour cream until well blended. Pour filling into chilled crust. Bake at 325° for 40-50 minutes. Filling will be soft & "jiggly" in the center, but it will set during cooling. Do not over bake! Cool thoroughly in spring form pan, at least 4 hours in refrigerator. Remove form, cut, serve and enjoy!

Serves 10-12

SERVING SUGGESTIONS:

This cheesecake is creamy and deliciously delicate, but thoroughly satisfying - with a fraction of the fat of other cheesecakes. You can top with cherries, apricot or raspberry sauce for a truly heavenly treat!

Cathy Myers
Dayspring Christian Academy
New Providence, Pennsylvania

Banana Oatmeal Cookies

INGREDIENTS:

3 cups flour
1 1/2 cups sugar
1 tsp. baking soda
1/2 tsp. nutmeg
1 1/2 tsp. cinnamon
1 1/2 cup apple sauce
1/2 cup Egg Beaters
2 cups mashed ripe banana
3 1/2 cups rolled oats
1/2 cup wheat germ (optional)

DIRECTIONS:

Mix together bananas, Egg Beaters & apple sauce. Sift together flour, sugar, baking soda, nutmeg & cinnamon & gradually add to banana mixture. Gradually add oatmeal & wheat germ & mix thoroughly. Drop by spoonfuls onto greased cookie sheets. Bake @ 400° 10 to 15 minutes. Immediately remove rack to cool.

Dee Crowe
BBC Striders
Belleville, Michigan

Good for You Pumpkin Pie

INGREDIENTS:

1/2 cup sugar
1/2 cup baking mix (Bisquick or Pioneer)
1 1/3 cup skim milk
2 eggs
1-16 oz. can pumpkin
2 1/2 tsp. pumpkin pie spice
2 tsp. vanilla

DIRECTIONS:

Heat oven to 350°. Spray pie plate with cooking oil. 10"x1 1/2" or 9"x1 1/4" pie plate. In a large bowl beat all ingredients on high speed with a hand mixer for 2 minutes. Pour into pie plate. Bake until golden brown and knife inserted in center comes out clean. Cooking time is approximately 60 minutes. Refrigerate any remaining pie.

SERVING SUGGESTIONS:

Great with a scoop of lowfat or fat free vanilla ice-cream.

Vicki Ralph
New Braunfels Running Club
New Braunfels, Texas

Low Fat Peach Bundt Cake

INGREDIENTS:

5 oz. low fat cake mix
4 cups diced peaches
3 cups peach juice
3 1/2 cups water
Topping:
12 cups drained, diced peaches
1/2 cup sugar
1 1/2 cup sugar free non-dairy topping

DIRECTIONS:

Preheat oven to 350°. Drain a 10 oz. can of peaches & save the juice. Pour 1/2 of juice & water into a mixing bowl, then add cake mix. Mix on low speed 1 minute. Scrape bowl & continue to mix on medium speed for 1 minute. Add remaining water & mix for 1 minute on low speed. Pour into bundt cake pan. Bake for 60-75 minutes in 350°oven. Let cool & slice each cake into 16 equal slices. Make topping by adding diced peaches & sugar and mixing well. Let set in cooler for 8-12 minutes. For best results make the day before & let set in cooler overnight. Place 2 oz. topping on each slice of cake & top with a dollop of sugar free whipped topping.

Executive Chef Richard Robinson
Provena Saint Joseph Medical Center Racing Heart
Joliet, Illinois

Mamie's Pound Cake

INGREDIENTS:

5 eggs
1 cup butter or margarine
1 3/4 cup sugar
2 cups flour
1 tsp. vanilla

DIRECTIONS:

Have eggs & butter at room temperature. Cream butter & sugar very well. Add unbeaten eggs alternately with flour. Add vanilla. Pour into well greased bundt pan. Bake for 1 hour in slow oven at 350°. Turn out while warm and get out the butter.

Shortly after we were engaged to be married, my fiance's parents were invited to have Sunday dinner with my family. My future mother-in-law's pound cake was always a welcome sight at social functions. So it was only appropriate that she bring one of these for dinner. The cake was never iced on any occasion. My oldest brother mistakenly thought that I had made it and throughout dinner he kept talking about anyone that would be so lazy to bring a cake with no icing. Everyone but him knew who had brought the cake and his wife kept kicking him under the table-to no avail. Mamie loved it and enjoyed watching him take his foot out of his mouth when it finally soaked in to him that it was her cake.

Susan Alexander
Mesa Monument Striders
Whitewater, Colorado

"Guilt-Free" Brownies

INGREDIENTS:

3 oz. unsweetened chopped chocolate
1 cup sugar
3/4 cup flour
3/4 cup (2%) low fat cottage cheese
3 egg whites
1 tsp. vanilla extract
1/4 tsp. salt

DIRECTIONS:

Melt chocolate over low heat, then cool slightly. Pureé other ingredients until smooth, then add chocolate. Pour into 8" square pan. Bake at 350° for 20-25 minutes or until just set. Sprinkle with powder sugar if desired.

Melaine R. Rudolph
Muncie, Indiana

Buckeye Candy

INGREDIENTS:

1 1/2 cups creamy peanut butter
1/2 cup (1 stick) softened butter
1 lb. confectioners sugar
1 tblsp. vanilla
Coating:
12 oz. pkg. chocolate chips

DIRECTIONS:

Mix all ingredients together with an electric mixer or by hand. Form into small balls, about 3/4" to 1" in size. Using a toothpick, dip balls into chocolate coating, leaving a small circle of peanut butter mixture uncoated to make them look like buckeyes. Place candy on waxed paper & chill until chocolate hardens. Candy can be frozen.

For chocolate coating melt chocolate chips in top of double boiler over hot water.

Buckeye candy is a tradition in Ohio. The official state tree is the Buckeye Tree and this candy is formed to resemble a Buckeye Nut(similar to a horse chestnut). It's a favorite during the fall season of OSU Football and the Columbus Marathon.

Makes about 4-5 dozen buckeye candies.

Joan Riegel
Columbus Marathon
Columbus, Ohio